Desperately Seeking Women Readers

Desperately Seeking Women Readers

U.S. Newspapers and the Construction of a Female Readership

Dustin Harp

LEXINGTON BOOKS

A division of
ROWMAN & LITTLEFIELD PUBLISHERS, INC.
Lanham • Boulder • New York • Toronto • Plymouth, UK

LEXINGTON BOOKS

A division of Rowman & Littlefield Publishers, Inc.
A wholly owned subsidiary of The Rowman & Littlefield Publishing Group, Inc.
4501 Forbes Boulevard, Suite 200
Lanham, MD 20706

Estover Road
Plymouth PL6 7PY
United Kingdom

Copyright © 2007 by Lexington Books

British Library Cataloguing in Publication Information Available

Library of Congress Cataloging-in-Publication Data

Harp, Dustin, 1968-
  Desperately seeking women readers : U.S. newspapers and the construction of a female
readership / Dustin Harp.
      p. cm.
  Includes bibliographical references and index.
  ISBN-13: 978-0-7391-1490-2 (cloth : alk. paper)
  ISBN-10: 0-7391-1490-5 (cloth : alk. paper)
  ISBN-13: 978-0-7391-1491-9 (pbk. : alk. paper)
  ISBN-10: 0-7391-1491-3 (pbk. : alk. paper)
  1. American newspapers—Sections, columns, etc.—Women—History—20th century.
I. Title.
  PN4888.W67H37 2007
  071'.3082--dc22   2007003072

Printed in the United States of America

♾™ The paper used in this publication meets the minimum requirements of American
National Standard for Information Sciences—Permanence of Paper for Printed Library
Materials, ANSI/NISO Z39.48–1992.

For my mothers and grandmothers—Joan, Anne, Maxine, and Joyce.

Contents

Part I

Introduction

Chapter 1
Newspapers, Women,
Social Movements, and Money

Women's pages in U.S. newspapers have a long history, beginning in the 1890s when newspaper publishers and editors in the United States introduced explicitly named sections to their female readers. This is not to say that prior to this time women did not read newspapers or find relevant and interesting material in them, but the 1890s is noted as the first time in which a general audience newspaper began creating entire sections of content specifically for women. Evidence indicates that in the decades leading to the unveiling of these newly developed sections, newspaper content increasingly attended to the desires of women and even children (Mott 1962). This was a likely result of daily newspaper publishers and editors noticing American women's devotion to women's magazines and newspapers published by and for women. The newly created women's pages and sections in general audience newspapers—typically not only designated for a female audience, but with titles that made this fact perfectly clear—have had a significant and long-lasting influence on the newspaper industry and how it has thought about and constructed women readers. Wanting readers to understand without a doubt that the content had been constructed for a female audience, publishers and editors of newspapers not only named these sections for women, but hired women to fill the space. These original women's sections contained content understood to fall within the feminine sphere, often summarized as subject matter occupying the "four Fs"—family, food, furnishings, and fashion. Society news, weddings, recipes, and advice columns also filled the pages of these traditional women's sections, as did news on women's changing roles in society and even feminist activism.

For eighty years the pages and sections devoted entirely to women appeared in newspapers throughout the country, until in January 1969, *The Washington Post* quit publishing women's pages and replaced them with a section meant for a broader audience. *The Post* dubbed the new section "Style." In July 1970, the *Los Angeles Times* moved in the same direction and debuted "View." Editors planned to integrate "women's content" into all areas of the newspaper and provide a lifestyle section of lighter, less timely news for a general readership. Industry leaders mark this time frame as the birth of modern-day feature sections (Mills 1988).

1

Following the lead of *The Washington Post* and *Los Angeles Times*, newspapers across the country stopped publishing explicitly named women's sections. The newly designed pages became known primarily as "style" or "lifestyle" sections and contained more entertainment and arts news (Guenin 1975). The conversion, editors claimed, was meant to attract diversified audiences into the world of "soft" news (Miller 1976). Much of the high-society news disappeared and content like weddings and club news—if included at all—became a minor part of lifestyle sections (a transformation that had been slowly happening in these "soft" news sections already). Important questions regarding this time in the newspaper industry concentrate on whether editors altered their gendered thinking about news content during this transition or simply changed the name of these sections. For example, did editors simply rename these sections or were they thinking about newspaper content beyond the male/female, hard/soft, news/feature dichotomies? Many argue the transition simply resulted in a name change and subtle shifts in content and not an adjustment in how newspaper editors conceptualized and constructed women readers.

Another turning point in the industry's thinking about female audiences came in the late 1980s when newspaper editors again started explicitly designating pages for women's content and a female readership. Through the 1990s the reintroduction of women's pages occurred in papers of all sizes and not just in small, hometown publications as some might expect. For example, one of the country's largest newspapers—the *Chicago Tribune*—started publishing a weekly section titled "Woman News." Some of the other newspapers to add these sex-specific sections during the 1990s include the *Lexington Herald-Leader* in Kentucky, *Arizona Republic*, *Cleveland Plain Dealer*, *Albuquerque Journal*, and *The Capital Times* in Madison, Wisconsin.

Rather than examine the content of women's pages, something a handful of studies have done, I consider industry and newsroom choices, changes, and practices to understand why and how women's pages developed and changed, and how those working on them have embraced and/or despised them. A purpose of this book is to illustrate how publishers, editors, and reporters in general audience newspapers have structured (or packaged) content for women and constructed a female audience. By examining the creation of women's pages and highlighting the significant turns in the industry throughout the decades, I show how these sections were developed not to create a more informed female audience but for advertisers wanting to reach women. Along with contextualizing the creation, elimination, and reintroduction of women's pages, a primary focus is to demonstrate how publishers, editors, and reporters conceptualize, construct, and regard the modern-day women's pages introduced in contemporary newsrooms of the 1990s. To accomplish this, the book offers interviews from within five newsrooms to better understand this sex-specific packaging of news and construction of women readers. By talking with those in the newsroom, the work illuminates the conditions that influence the construction of news work while offering insight into the topic from the very people who have implemented the rebirth of women's pages. Through this type of face-to-face investigation an understanding of why and how these pages have been (re)produced and the complexities and contradictions surrounding them materializes. But more than look at newspapers and their relationship with women readers, this research speaks to broader issues of newspaper marketing. While showing how newspapers specifically target women readers, the information gathered for this book illustrates how market concerns drive the presentation and packaging of newspaper content.

While this book attends at its perimeters to the content of women's pages, it is not a systematic analysis of content. I do, however, discuss the stories and topics that appear in these sections. My knowledge of the content of these women's sections is informed by previous research, direct descriptions from those who have produced the content, and my unsystematic but informed readings of these sections. So while I do not present an analysis of content in these sections, I do talk about the content in regard to direct examples presented by those who have produced them. Rather than gain insight into the nuances of content, this investigation concentrates on content topics, who defines women's news content, and who constructs—or defines—the female reader. In other words, instead of investigating the content of stories about women, this book explores how both an industry and specific newspaper publishers, editors, and reporters have packaged and constructed a set of texts for women. In doing this, I illustrate how newspaper publishers and editors help to establish and reinforce binary conceptions of newspaper content. That is to say, how practices in the industry have instituted and reinforced the male/female, hard/soft, news/feature dichotomies still present in many contemporary newsrooms and newspapers. Further, I expose the contradictions inherent in constructing and packaging content for women and the implications inherent in designating news content for a particular sex.

Beyond an investigation of the newspaper industry, I am concerned with the effects of social structure and media systems on patterns of news content. The approach moves beyond the individual and the news industry and takes into account the newsmakers sense of their audience and the entire ideological atmosphere of our society as the filter through which news is constructed (Schudson 1989). This book begins with the proposition that newspapers (and the packaging of news texts) are constructed within a complex social system and both reflect and reinforce cultural realities, values, and beliefs. Newspapers—from individual stories to pages and sections—form a socially constructed picture of the world and not one that is real and natural. Both how news content is constructed and how it is packaged is important. These texts produced in newsrooms are cultural objects that generate and circulate meanings (Fiske 1992). This book focuses on industry decisions about the packaging and marketing of news texts to understand the role of women's and style pages in the cultural construction of meanings about women and gender. Through an investigation of the production of women's pages in American newspapers this study illuminates the news media's contribution to and reinforcement of the construction of women and their marginal position in society.

I consider not only a tension between newspapers and women readers but reflect on a broader social friction concerning women and their proper place in society. Ultimately, the book contemplates the meaning and effects of marginalizing "women's news" into one section of a newspaper. The issue is more complex than one might imagine as these sections have both served and "ghettoized" women, as producers and readers of news. On the one hand they have offered women entry into journalism and the newspaper industry. These pages have also allowed women access to define news because they have functioned as editors of women's pages. In other areas of the newspaper, women have had fewer opportunities to serve in editorial positions, particularly in the early history of the industry. This ability for women to choose news has meant that serious stories seen as unimportant to male editors—stories that would not have been in the newspaper otherwise—have been published and read. At the same time, however, women's pages have impeded women reporters' progress for advancement in the newsroom, as women have often been relegated to these subsections of the paper and not allowed to write for the front pages where stories about politics, the legal system, and war reside. Women's sections and the marginalization of "women's news" indicate to newspaper readers that certain topics are of interest to women and are not of importance to men. To complicate matters more, many women enjoy reading these sections and are not bothered by the sex-specific intention behind their production.

This book also considers broadly how feminist movements have responded over the decades to women's pages and the separation of "women's news." There is evidence indicating the women's movement of the 1960s and 1970s influenced the termination of women's sections during that time. But how did feminist thinkers respond to the original creation of these sections and the eventual return of women's pages in the 1990s? Understanding why and how the production of women's sections could be embraced by a community in the 1990s when only years earlier that community had named them sexist and had demanded their termination offers insight into cultural attitudes about women, the women's movement, and feminisms during the end of the twentieth century. I consider the introduction of contemporary women's sections as an illustration of broader and more complex debates about gender equality, women's roles in society, and the "marginalization" of women that critics of these sections say they reflect. This reflection offers insight into how women and men understand themselves and their position in contemporary U.S. society.

This investigation fills an important gap in research concerning women and newspapers. While it is indebted to those relatively few who have studied women in journalism, it also builds on their work by chronicling contemporary changes in the newspaper industry's construction of their female readers. Through the words of contemporary news workers, this volume ensures the preservation of newsroom perceptions and judgments about women readers during a particularly interesting time in the history of women and journalism.

The Business of News, Advertising, and Consumerism

That a newspaper's primary goal is to inform citizens about the community and world where they live is an ideal but inaccurate notion. Regardless of the intentions of those who produce news, the bottom line is that newspaper publishers must rely on revenue, primarily in the form of advertisers and to a lesser extent from their audience. Women's pages in the 1890s were not altruistically developed out of a concern for women and their need for information but to secure a group of readers that could be delivered to advertisers. Newspapers' survival then as now depends on revenue generated by advertising. This reliance on advertising essentially began in the late 1890s when industrialization brought with it a need to sell the wealth of products being produced. But newspaper advertisers were and are not simply interested in reaching the widest audience possible, they are concerned with attracting those people who are most likely to buy their goods and services. Because of this pressure for newspapers to not just deliver an audience for advertisements but to provide access to potential buyers for advertised products, newspapers (as well as other forms of mass media) developed target audiences.

A target audience is defined by such attributes as age, gender, income, attitudes, and lifestyle and is deemed the most likely audience to buy particular products (Fost 1991). To draw target audiences into a newspaper publishers and editors continually evaluate content and readership demographics, and then add and reconfigure content so that it will appeal to desirable readers. In fact, substantial evidence exists illustrating how both directly and indirectly advertisers influence media content (Shoemaker and Reese 1991). By the 1890s women had become the primary decision-makers in how families spend their money, choosing which food, clothing, and household goods to purchase. Women's pages offered advertisers, including those who were promoting the developing department stores, a direct link to these women and are one of the clearest and earliest examples of U.S. newspaper publishers' and editors' efforts to reconstruct content to acquire and maintain specific readers. This book illustrates clearly the marketing concerns within the newspaper industry.

Constructing Meaning, Constructing Gender

A significant area of mass communication research notes journalism's role in not only the dissemination of information, but also the construction of meaning within a society (Carragee 1991). Danner and Walsh (1999) write that "how women and women's issues are covered in mainstream U.S. media is representative of a more insidious trend in media (and American society generally) that covertly and continuously emphasizes the ideology of white males as the dominant group in American society" (64). Typically researchers in this area refer to the particulars of texts or sets of texts and not where these texts are placed in newspapers or the ways in which news is divided and presented within newspapers. How individual texts are presented within a newspaper or specifically how content by, for, and about women is packaged, however, conveys and circulates information and can indicate broader issues about women's place in society.

In "Hearth and Home" the authors explain, "Americans learn basic lessons about social life from the mass media," (Tuchman et al. 1978, 3). About women and the media, the authors offer two useful ideas. First the "reflection hypothesis" that claims "the mass media reflect dominant societal values" and, second, "symbolic annihilation," which is the "condemnation, trivialization or absence" of women (Tuchman et al. 1978, 7–8). These are constructive concepts to consider in relation to newspapers and the packaging of sex-specific content. With these concepts in mind, a number of questions direct the course of this book. What basic lessons can be learned about social life when newspaper content considered of interest to women is placed in a separate section, away from the front page news and apart from the sports sections and business pages? What messages does this content construction convey about gender? Does this separation of content reflect dominant societal values? What does the division of content say about women and men's roles in the public and private spheres? Does it trivialize women's interests and women's lives? And, when newspaper editors construct a section for women, does it result in a narrow definition of women?

The binary notion of news content that was developed/reinforced in the earliest women's pages is often described as "soft" and "hard" news. Since its inception, however, this distinction has proven ambiguous (Tuchman 1978). Most often, editors and reporters define "soft" news as that which is interesting, mostly "because it deals with the life of human beings" (Tuchman 1978, 48). "Hard" news, in contrast, includes news that is "important." This begs the question: Important to whom? An examination into content in women's pages throughout the decades illustrates a variety of stories that can be described as either interesting and/or important. As Tuchman (1978) points out after observing the production of news in the 1970s, "it is difficult, if not impossible, to decide whether an event is interesting or important or is both interesting and important" (48). Hartley (1982) points to the sexist nature of this distinction, explaining that soft news stories are "often defined as having a 'woman's angle'" and are characterized as "fluff" while hard news is typically characterized by conflict and violence (38). Mills (1988) notes about the distinction: "Hard news? Soft news? Where did these terms come from? Their sexual implications fairly leap from the pages" (110). The hard/soft line has been drawn on the basis of stereotypical notions of women and men—feminine and masculine, which parallels a distinction between the public and private spheres (Yang 1996). Women's newspaper content starting in the nineteenth century, guided in no small part by content in already-established women's magazines, focused on the domestic/private sphere that women of the time were expected to occupy. News concerning institutions occupying the public sphere (government, law, and the economy) were defined as men's or "hard" news and filled the main pages of newspapers. This move in newspapers away from the strictly serious and to lighter content has been described as the "feminization" of the press and, some argue, has been replicated in broadcast news through the growing use of female anchors (Holland 1998; van Zoonen 1994).

Feminist Ideologies

While this book does not attempt to trace feminism as a social movement, in looking at the newspaper industry's reevaluation of women readers over time, I consider social and ideological shifts and the ways in which dominant and alternative ideologies may have influenced industry changes. Understanding the role of women and the social context within which women's pages have existed in the United States may offer an explanation for why versions of these texts have existed at times and ceased to exist at other times during the history of U.S. newspapers. In other words, it may offer clues as to how alternative (feminist) ideologies have influenced the industry's construction of women readers. Concepts of ideology and hegemony theory are useful in this endeavor to understand what drove the introduction, re-evaluation, and reintroduction of women's pages in U.S. newspapers. These ideas offer a way to think about mass communications' role in constructing reality and reinforcing cultural norms while also offering a means with which to understand how struggles over meaning occur within societies. From this critical perspective the media industry represents a place where ideological struggles play out, through the production of content and presentation of events and issues as the "norm" versus a socially constructed reality. As I evaluate the changes in the newspaper industry, I grapple with ways in which alternative feminist ideologies confront, struggle against, and win and lose ground to dominant ideologies both within and outside of the news industry. Further I show the complexity of feminist ideologies, illustrated by the ways in which women's pages have both been embraced and criticized in the name of feminist ideals.

Becker (1984) offers an especially useful way to understand ideology within the framework of this book. He explains that it is "an integrated set of frames of reference through which each of us sees the world and to which all of us adjust our actions" (Becker 1984, 69). Becker's definition points out how ideologies not only offer people a way in which to make sense of their world, but also includes how these ideologies influence our world—by causing people to adjust their actions. The second part of Becker's definition offers a way to think beyond dominant and alternative ideologies as sets of beliefs and to think about how these beliefs influence industry and newsroom practices and how news producers function ideologically. Hegemony theory offers a way to conceptualize the negotiation that takes place between alternative feminist ideologies that both argue for and against the segregation of women's news content and a dominant ideology that values patriarchal and capitalist ideals. Hegemony, a term originally conceptualized by Gramsci, attends to the constant struggle over meaning and power within a society. "Hegemony characterizes social relations as a series of struggles for power," a way in which the dominant ideology "can be resisted, evaded, or negotiated" (Fiske 1987, 41). These two concepts attend to the complex nature of how "news texts routinely emphasize meanings and values associated with those groups, which hold positions of political and economic power" while recognizing "ideological inconsistencies and contradictions within" the news (Carragee 1991, 3). The negotiation or constant struggle over meaning explained through hegemonic theory is particularly relevant in reference to women's sections in U.S. newspapers. These sex-specific sections in newspapers are contradictory. The pages often offer women important and desired content but also segregate and essentialize women's concerns, while telling men that they need not worry about issues like childcare, rape laws, and abortion.

Feminist scholars point to a dominant ideology in Western culture based on patriarchy, white supremacy, and capitalist values—ideals that situate men, whiteness, and economic gain above other positions (Ryan 1992). Because of the news media's ability to both reflect and construct social reality, this dominant ideology influences media content in often unexamined ways. Feminisms and feminist media theories offer a set of beliefs and explanations that counter the powerful dominant system of thinking and attempt to emancipate traditionally oppressed people. Because ideology as understood through hegemony theory is never static and always changing, feminist beliefs to varying degrees and at specific times have become "common sense" cultural realities that have become absorbed into the dominant ideology. For example, at one time in U.S. history women were barred from voting because they were not thought to be autonomous beings (Ryan 1992). Eventually this limited notion of women came to be seen as invalid and now few question women's right to vote. This example illustrates the instability of the dominant ideology and how competing or alternative ideologies become part of an ever-changing common-sense way of thinking. This book examines the role alternative feminist ideologies may have played in the newspaper industry's construction of female readers.

To overlay feminist ideologies onto the decisions of the U.S. newspaper industry over space and time necessitates an understanding of American feminisms. This, however, is a daunting task as both feminist media theories and U.S. feminisms occupy a complex and contested terrain. Authors write entire books on the subject so the discussion here will inevitably be incomplete. The goal, however, is to offer an understanding of feminisms during the key moments of the construction and (re)construction of female readers that I identify within the newspaper industry from the 1890s through the start of the twenty-first century. The attention to feminisms in relation to this book, in other words, is not with the intention of thoroughly defining them, but rather in articulating if or how tenets of feminism might have influenced newspapers' packaging of content for women. My discussion of feminisms then is presented with an understanding of the incomplete nature of such a condensed version but a belief that I touch on main tenets and (re)articulations and offer a way in which to understand the changing newspaper industry's construction of women readers and the contradictory and complex roles feminisms have played.

Feminism and the women's movement, like any social and political movement, have a long and complicated history. It is best understood as a complex political movement, one in which the defining characteristics have continually changed and are often at the center of intense debate both within academic and activist communities. This multiplicity of perspectives explains why I use feminisms in the plural, as there are various tenets of thought. Feminist movements in the United States have most often been delineated into waves of activity, with the first wave coinciding with the introduction of explicitly named women's pages into U.S. newspapers.

The 1848 Seneca Falls Convention in New York marks the nations first women's rights convention. There were three-hundred women and men in attendance (Krolokke and Sorensen 2006). At the convention a declaration outlined by Elizabeth Cady Stanton declared women's natural equality and political strategies for gaining equal opportunities and access (Donovan 1994). Referred to as first-wave feminism, the movement dedicated itself primarily to the suffrage movement, though reform movements such as temperance and abolition also occupied the movement's attention (Ryan 1992). First-wave feminists challenged stereotypes of women and the ways in which women of the time were expected to behave. Among these prominent beliefs about women: they were weak, incompetent, and expected to be pure. A problem with first-wave feminism, however, was that while some women of color participated in the movement, for the most part the movement consisted of white, middle-class, well-educated women. The two main tenets of first-wave U.S. feminism are often referred to as liberal feminism and socialist/Marxist feminism, developed in workers' unions. Liberal feminists accept biological differences but do not accept them as theoretically or politically valid reasons for discrimination. Both liberal and socialist/Marxist feminism "shared a basic belief in equity and equal opportunity for women and men, but the latter focused particularly on working-class women and their involvement in class struggle and socialist revolution" (Krolokke and Sorensen 2006, 6).

The first-wave feminist movement in the United States remained relatively strong until women finally won the right to vote in 1920. But with the victory of the vote, the unifying issue of the movement was gone. It was then that the "various sectors dissipated into separate issues divided by two opposing views: one calling for women's equality and the other for women's protections" (Ryan 1992, 34). The debate questioned whether women should work for advancement as people in their own right, or whether women, as mothers, needed special treatment to fulfill this role. This debate proved a monumental dividing point for the movement—one that still has relevancy today. The result: while various women's organizations were interested in improving women's social status, the lack of a cohesive ideology resulted in what could be perceived as a reduced feminist presence within U.S. society. Women's pages in U.S. newspapers were introduced to readers during this first wave of feminism, a time when women had limited rights and little access to the newspaper industry. In fact, women and feminists of the time could easily have understood these newly developed pages in a positive light as they offered women opportunities for a public voice despite reinforcing gender stereotypes. I have found no evidence indicating women's aversion to these newly developed newspaper sections but can surmise that feminists may have had mixed reactions to them as they both offered women opportunities and reinforced stereotypes.

In contemporary terms, second-wave feminism identifies organization and activity during the 1960s and 1970s. This rebirth of feminism is typically understood to be a reaction to the family-centered years of the 1950s (Ryan 1992). Women had moved in great numbers into paid employment during World War II but the era following the war is marked with an ideological shift that re-established women's place in the home and "defined the wife/mother role as both women's special duty and path to fulfillment" (Ryan 1992, 42). The focus and participation of this more radical second-wave feminism was much broader than the first. It also cannot be separated from other leftist movements of the time from which it grew, including the anti-Vietnam War movement and civil rights movement. The revitalized women's movement concerned itself with the "transformation of society on the social, political, economic, spiritual, personal, interactional, and cultural levels" and stressed the need to address difference (Ryan 1992, 40). The difference, however, was limited to men and women and attended less to differences between women. For this reason, second-wave feminism has been criticized for exclusionary and simplistic notions of women. Contemporary (or third-wave) feminists argue that second-wave feminism was made up of and concerned itself with white, upper middle-class, heterosexual women. Specific issues of concern included domestic violence, employment and educational opportunities, wage discrimination, rape laws, and sexual violence. Not only did feminism focus on a variety of issues, by the early 1970s the feminist movement had become fragmented into more distinct orientations—among the most visible: radical feminists, socialist feminists, and liberal feminists (Ryan 1992).

Regardless of the fragmentation of feminist ideologies during this time, a number of significant cultural changes regarding women and gender occurred. In no small part because together women demanded changes. The transformations focused on the public aspects of society (versus the domestic sphere) and included a number of challenges and changes within the newspaper industry. Title VII of the 1964 Civil Rights Act, which outlawed discrimination in employment on the basis of gender, along with the sheer numbers of women working and studying outside the home, made the challenges to existing social structures easier. Inside the news industry women were asking for equal opportunities to cover all news and equal pay for their work. And when asking was not enough, women turned to the Equal Employment Opportunity Commission and the courts. During the 1970s women at the Wire Service Guild filed a discrimination complaint against the Associated Press, claiming unfair pay and assignments. Women at *The Washington Post* did the same, while women at *The New York Times* filed a lawsuit in a U.S. District Court (Beasley and Gibbons 2003). Each of these cases helped women to gain ground in the journalism industry.

During this cultural climate it does not seem surprising that newspaper editors began changing the way they packaged news for women. The transition within the newspaper industry that occurred in the 1960s and early 1970s clearly happened during a time of renewed feminist activism across the country. The time was one of both ideological shifts and changes in social realities, and included women's movement into the workforce — and newsrooms—at a much higher rate than ever before. With this shift, women journalists made heard inside newsrooms what others outside the newsroom were declaring—that women's pages segregated and marginalized women's concerns and ultimately deemed them less important than those issues covered on the front pages. Further, critics argued that by naming one section of the newspaper for women, newspaper editors indicated that the rest of the newspaper was constructed for men. By extension, that meant men—and not women—were concerned with and responsible for the serious issues found on the front pages of newspapers, including stories about politics, economics, and foreign affairs. But while many newspaper publishers and editors acknowledged the criticism others simply renamed the sex-specific pages.

During the late 1970s and early 1980s a drive to pass the Equal Rights Amendment (ERA) offered a cause to unite feminist activists. But the ERA also presented anti-feminists a cause. Ryan (1992) explains, "During the latter part of the 1970s and the early 1980s the U.S. women's movement felt the effects of the anti-feminist backlash and a growing conservative climate" (97). By the mid-1980s, a decade characterized by the rise of conservatism, the intensity of second-wave feminism had been replaced by an anti-feminist ideology. In *Backlash: The Undeclared War against American Women*, Faludi (1991) details contemporary American social, political, and economic institutions during the 1980s to reveal what she names a covert movement "to remind women to embrace traditional roles or suffer the consequences" (80). This backlash thesis has gained popularity by many who believe throughout the last twenty-five years women have lost ground in their fight for equality. Faludi (1991) argued, "the last decade has seen a powerful counterassault on women's rights, a backlash, an attempt to retract the handful of small and hard-won victories that the feminist movement did manage to win for women" (xviii). While acknowledging this assault on feminism is not organized, she points to the resurgence of conservatism—and its "family values" rhetoric—as a primary agitator of the backlash. Of particular interest to communication scholars is Faludi's detailing of U.S. news media's role in perpetuating this backlash. She argues the news media contribute to the backlash through its reporting on it. She explains how repeatedly the backlash theme emerged in the press: women have achieved so much but are so miserable (Faludi 1991).

In considering the reintroducing of women's pages, this book considers whether contemporary women's pages are another example of the feminist backlash in the U.S. news media.

Some feminist theorists, however, have criticized Faludi's thesis, maintaining that her argument is overly reductive and pessimistic (Rapping 1994). Countering Faludi's contention, Rapping argues that during the last two decades mass media has responded to feminism in positive ways. Investigations into soap operas, television, and films have shown how these forms of mass communication have addressed issues that feminists have placed on the national agenda, including rape, domestic violence, incest, economic issues, and discrimination (Cuklanz 1996; Rapping 1994). Rapping calls for a less monolithic attack on mass media, one that takes into account the nuances and contradictions of media content. Within the context of Rapping's criticism of Faludi, the reintroduction of women's pages cannot simply be seen as a way of reminding women of their "marginalized" place in society. Media texts, including women's pages, are full of inconsistencies and can not be referred to in monolithic terms, especially when considering how ideologies—including both a dominant patriarchal and alternative feminist ideologies—influence the construction of texts and meaning. These contemporary debates offer a framework within which to understand feminism's relationship to the production of contemporary women's sections, newspapers, and mass media in general. These disputes within feminist media theories also are indicative of the varied tensions and tenets within contemporary or third wave feminisms.

Contemporary feminists encounter debates over the need for a women's movement. Some argue this is because recent generations of women avoid the "feminist" label as they enjoy hard-won opportunities in education and careers and lack historical insight into the women's equality movement. The time has been marked by some who point to a third wave of feminism and others who have hinted at an end to the women's movement. Much of the contemporary debate centers on the need and relevance of feminism in contemporary times (Faludi 1991). Many feminists argue the solution is for a new generation of women to redefine issues and needs central to a contemporary feminism. This is happening. The women's movement of today proves much more complicated and fractured—in no small part as a result of the perceived (or real) exclusionary practices of the second wave. But while diverse, third wave feminisms share a desire to "redefine feminism by bringing together an interest in traditional and even stereotypical feminine issues, while remaining critical of both narratives of true femaleness, of victimization and liberation" (Krolokke and Sorensen 2006, 17).

This discussion of American feminism, albeit cursory, offers a way in which to think about alternative feminist and dominant ideologies as they may have influenced or been influenced by the newspaper industry's construction of women readers. The number of referential terms offers an indication of the varied perspectives, goals, and tenets within the women's movement but the fundamental ideology underlying feminist thought regardless of the feminism under question is a desire for improving the conditions of women (Ryan 1992). Within the context of this discussion, it is especially interesting to consider the rebirth of women's pages in the newspaper industry during the late 1980s and early 1990s. What conditions allowed these sections that had been eliminated more than thirty years earlier to come back?

Women in Journalism

Women's inability to define news and move issues of importance to women onto the front pages has been limited by women's roles in society but also, significantly, by their positions in the media industry. Men, primarily white men, have long dominated newsroom editorial boards so not only have they shaped news from outside of the industry but defined it from within. Throughout the history of newspapers women have been relatively absent in positions of power except as editors of women's sections. This has meant women have had little say in defining news and what is important and, in turn, have had little hand in the construction of reality. In other words, in significant ways through their lack of public voice women have been denied access to shape notions of gender and what it means to be a woman. Critics of the industry argue that the news treatment of women (and minorities) will not change until women in greater numbers assume decision-making positions in news organizations (van Zoonen 1994). Scholars investigating women's roles in U.S. newspapers have chronicled how women reporters' have attempted to break free of assumptions and parochial limitations, define news, and change coverage of women (Beasley and Gibbons 2003; Marzolf 1977; Mills 1988). One place they have done this is in women's alternative media outlets. Throughout history, however, most of this shaping of news content in mainstream newspapers has taken place on women's pages where women actually have had editorial power.

Disagreement exists about whether news would really change if women served in decision-making positions within newsrooms. Some critics of the industry argue that because of their unique position in U.S. society, women have a unique perspective that, had they the opportunity, would affect news content. The argument is based on a belief that women generally experience life differently than men because, among other reasons, they are typically the primary care givers and homemakers in American culture. But van Zoonen points out two problematic assumptions occupying this position: first that journalists have the agency to perform in an individual manner; and second "that female journalists are distinguished more by their femininity than by any other dimension of identity, like professionalism or ethnicity" (van Zoonen 1998). So while some argue that women in newsrooms will make a difference, because of their unique life experiences and perspectives, other communication researchers argue that individual characteristics like gender are overpowered by news routines and organizational policy. Others point out an essentialist and universalizing notion of women built into the argument that women and men construct news differently based on their gender. Research in this area is mixed with some illustrating differences between men and women editors (Merritt and Gross 1978). These found differences, however, are not always present in research findings, a point that illuminates the complexities of journalists and the newsrooms in which they work. Mills (1988) shows how women in newsrooms have affected news content:

> Simply put, the presence of more women in the newsroom has changed some attitudes of their male editors. The presence of more women covering stories has led to more women being interviewed. Many men see only men as subjects for quotation while women, who are used to listening to both women and men, interview both women and men as a matter of course. The presence of more women (not many more but more) editing stories has given some reporters pause before they described a woman's physical attributes or marital status. How relevant were those, after all? The presence of some women on assignment desks has meant that stories about rape-law reform, abortion, and sexual harassment and about local women who are politicians might get straight news treatment. (10)

Those who are skeptical of the idea that women will change news point to the organizational restraints and the norms, values, and routines that journalists learn in the newsroom. In line with this thinking, many media critics have focused on how women and ethnic minorities in the news industry, who often express dissatisfaction with news coverage related to their groups, conform to organizational policies (Tuchman 1978). Studies have looked at the organizational restraints that have lead many women reporters and the few women editors to reproduce news as it has always been produced. Liebler and Smith (1997) investigated male and female network news correspondents to learn whether they reported events comparably or whether gender differences played a role in diversifying news content. The authors found organizational constraints at work and concluded "although women may constitute a critical mass in network newsrooms, their presence has seemingly little impact on the way news is reported" (Liebler and Smith 1997, 65). This book considers these various perspectives on women's role and possible influence on news content as it contemplates the acceptability of women's segregated content and their marginalization in newsrooms.

Outline of Book

This book offers a detailed analysis of how the newspaper industry in the United States has constructed a female audience through the creation, termination, and restoration of women's pages and sections. It details external and internal conditions that lead those in the newspaper industry to initially begin offering women pages of their own, while also exploring how these traditional sections were constructed over several decades. It further analyzes the influences that directed the industry to abandon women's pages during the 1960s and 1970s and finally focuses on the rebirth of women's pages during the late 1980s and throughout the 1990s. To understand the early history of women's pages in U.S. newspapers, the study relies primarily on published histories of women in newspapers and published interviews of women who have played a part in the newspaper industry. While the number of histories specifically addressing women and women's pages in U.S. newspapers is relatively small, those that do exist together offer a way to assemble and verify the past. More opportunities for learning about the recent history of women's pages exist. Not only are there published research projects, interviews, and articles from industry magazines and newspapers, there is an opportunity to talk with those who have been involved in the recreation of these pages. I conducted face-to-face, in-depth interviews with thirty-five journalists at five newspapers to gain an understanding of how contemporary newspapers construct women readers or why they choose not to.

Chapter two details the early history of women's pages, from the 1890s through the 1950s. In the chapter I rely on key texts related to the history of women and newspapers. More recent texts related to women and contemporary journalism issues also filled in details. Where possible, several texts were compared to ensure the accurate reporting of events. Further, when the cross comparison of sources proved contradictory, both versions were reported unless other sources presented an opportunity to verify the accuracy of events. I focus on the transition from women's pages to style sections in chapter three. Rather than simply describe the transition in the way I detail the history of women's pages in the previous chapter, I offer an analysis of articles published in industry trade journals during the time. Through this analysis I provide an in-depth discussion of the ways in which those working in the industry perceived the reconstruction of women's pages into non-sex–specific style pages. This research adds to a handful of important existing works about the termination of traditional women's pages and the industry's transition to style pages (Guenin 1975; Miller 1976; Yang 1996). The value of this examination is its ability to illuminate a discussion that existed during a specific time in the industry's history and identify the perspectives of those in the industry during a time when structuring of news content and the construction of a female audience changed. This restructuring is important to study because it indicates a theoretically critical moment in the relationship between women and the production of news. I use the word "theoretically" to highlight the contested notion of change during this time—one that arguably happened in name only.

Chapters four through seven focus on the contemporary turn back to women's pages in the newspaper industry. To understand the reinstitution of women's sections during the 1990s, I interviewed news workers in five newspapers, including three that had by 2000 embraced new specifically named women's pages—the *Chicago Tribune, The Capital Times* (Madison, Wisconsin), and the *Lexington Herald-Leader* (Kentucky). I also conducted interviews at two newspapers without explicitly named women's pages—the *Milwaukee Journal Sentinel* and *Wis-*

consin State Journal. While chapter four focuses on the contemporary turn, the following three chapters are thematic, providing a depth of material to better understand how contemporary women's pages have been conceptualized, constructed, and resisted. Chapter five specifically addresses how publishers, editors, and other journalists define women's news and construct women's pages. In chapter six I show the contradictions that arise in newsrooms were these contemporary women's pages are produced, and how often women in these newsrooms disagree with producing them. In chapter seven, I present interviews from two newsroom that have resisted naming content by sex. In this chapter I also offer an argument for diversifying newsrooms, one based on my talks with the thirty-five journalists I spoke with. This chapter is followed by the conclusion. In summarizing the book in the final chapter I argue against the explicit separation and naming of newspaper content for women. While acknowledging the many areas of mass communication specifically targeting an audience based on sex or gender, I argue that the charge of news organizations is unique in its mission to inform a democracy. Because of this, newspaper editors should attempt to integrate news of interest to all citizens in all areas of their papers.

Finally, before proceeding, I have some notes about the terms and language I use. I use the term "sex-specific" rather than "gender-specific" to highlight the narrow designation of women's pages, one based on the binary concept of men and women. I want to point out the difference between the biological term "woman" and a culturally constructed notion of woman, which is gender. While I believe the sections construct a conception of woman, one that changes over time, publishers and editors are designating their audience using a biological term that essentializes and constructs gender ideals. Also, throughout the book the phrase "women's pages" and "women's sections" are used interchangeably. Newspaper editors have taken different approaches when constructing gender specific content, some producing an entire section and others offering pages within a section. Rather than the number of pages or whether the pages stand alone as a unique section does not change their designation. When speaking about women's sections or pages, what this book is referring to are pages and sections with titles or subtitles that explicitly identify the target readership. For example: "Woman News" or "News for Today's Women." I do, also, acknowledge how the turn to style pages may not have actually changed much in the eyes of publishers, editors, or even readers. I explore this but when I talk of these newly developed sections I will refer to them as style or lifestyle sections and not women's pages. Throughout this book, an underlying grand question is whether or not the name of a section or sex-specific designation of pages really matters. After all, if the intended audience is the same in the eyes of publishers, editors, and reporters, what difference does the name make? In fact as I worked on this project I often thought of the famous line in William Shakespeare's Romeo and Juliet: "What is in a name? That which we call a rose by any other word would smell as sweet " (Shakespeare 2006).

Part II

The History of Women's Pages

Chapter 2
Introducing "Women's News"

During the second half of the nineteenth century American newspapers experienced an increased readership. A number of factors contributed, including a developing public education, a price drop in the production and distribution of newspapers, and more women readers. Tapping into the interests of this female readership, newspaper executives began introducing specifically constructed women's pages in large U.S. newspapers during the 1890s. But the motives behind attracting women readers to newspapers had more to do with marketing and business and much less to do with the altruistic notion of informing the other sex about daily public life. This was a time, after all, when women were still kept from political life and largely confined to the private sphere of home and family, a time when women were still forbidden to cast a vote in political elections. From the perspective of publishers, editors, and reporters—overwhelmingly men—and considering women's position in society, it seemed understandable that women might need alternative content to that found on the front pages. Content concentrating on the feminine realm seemed the natural way to draw in and keep women reading the newspaper. This mission was especially important to newspaper executives because women readers were exactly who advertisers in the last part of the nineteenth century were most interested in reaching.

Marketing to Women

Newspaper publishers' plan to construct reading material specifically for women did not qualify as novel. In fact the concept came straight from women's magazines, which gained popularity in the decades prior to the formal introduction of women's pages in general newspapers. The history of these magazines adds details to a story about women in the United States and how they have been positioned as the primary consumers in a capitalist culture. Understanding how these magazines were established and the motivations behind their production helps explain the newspaper industry's move toward female-targeted content.

Periodicals targeting women and ultimately serving as both a definer of and adviser for femininity and domesticity in the United States go back to 1792 with the short-lived *The Lady's Magazine and Repository of Entertaining Knowledge*

(Zuckerman 1998). By the time the American Civil War began more than one hundred of these publications existed, with the best known being Godey's *Lady's Book* (Zukerman 1998; Endres and Lueck 1995). While these early women's magazines carried some of the same types of content—etiquette and fashion—as those created after the Civil War, they were different in that they targeted an elite class of women, had few if any advertising within their pages, and were relatively costly. Godey's, which at its peak in the 1860s reached a circulation of one-hundred-fifty thousand, presented content to a readership that was upper to upper-middle class (Walker 2000). The pages included sketches of the latest fashions but were devoid of practical advice since the targeted readers were assumed to have servants who tended to household duties.

By the end of the war in 1865 and through the remaining part of the nineteenth century, however, a number of technological and social changes resulted in a new breed of women's periodicals more closely related to the mass marketed women's magazines of today. Directly affecting the magazine industry were innovations in printing technology, which made the production, and in turn the product, less costly. Magazine distribution became easier too because of a number of changes, including the railroad system, better roads, and a less costly postal service (Zuckerman 1998). The symbiotic relationship between magazine publishers and advertisers developed during this time as well, when many more ads began to appear and many of the strategies still utilized today were first developed. Among the new developments, magazine editors distributed advertising throughout their pages rather than relegating it to the back and began positioning advertising near related editorial content (Zuckerman 1998). Department store ads and national advertising, which experienced an enormous rise from 1890 to 1917, had an impact on women's magazines as well (Mott 1962; Zuckerman 1998).

At this same time urbanization and industrialization were increasing at a rapid pace. People were moving from the country to the city and from farm work to factory production. Consequently the notion of work and home/family life became separated as industrialization moved production out of the domestic sphere for the middle-class urban family. Labor within and outside the home became more clearly divided than ever before and this differentiation of the family from the economy resulted in changing roles within the family (Oakley 1974). From this emerged the modern housewife. Sociologist Ann Oakley (1974) calls the emergence of this dominant role "the most important and enduring consequence of industrialization for women" (32). Housework, child rearing, and shopping for household goods and necessities were considered the responsibilities of the housewife/woman. But this reality meant different things to different women, as the changes resulting from the movement into cities and factory work did not affect all women equally. For immigrant and lower-class women industrialization and urbanization meant working outside the home in factories and in the homes of upper-class women as well as working inside the home. For a wealthier class of women, these social transformations allowed for more leisure activities, increased

access to education, and opportunities for social activism and professional interests. For magazine publishers this latter group of women represented an expanded
readership.

The expansion of the middle class not only had tangible effects on women,
it also influenced the ideological constructions of women that were presented
and reinforced in magazines. Now more women were being defined and defining
themselves by idealized virtues upon which middle- and upper-class women were
expected to maintain prior to the shifting social landscape. These virtues, based
upon principles rooted in the Victorian period, framed the ideal woman in the
home as wife and mother (Abramson 1990). Historian Barbara Welter identified
four ideals of the Victorian era that women were expected to adhere to—piety,
purity, submissiveness, and domesticity—and named these constructed expectations the "Cult of True Womanhood" (Welter 1966). Expectations of domesticity
reinforced the role of the modern housewife and a woman's place in the home as
a wife and mother. This notion of a woman's true nature and place in society constructed, reinforced, and naturalized the public/private male/female dichotomies.
The result was a strengthening of the idea that men were naturally meant to occupy the public arena while women tended to the private/domestic sphere. Within
this private sphere women were expected to behave a certain way. This dominant
ideological understanding of ideal womanhood formed a guide for women's place
and behavior in U.S. culture. The magazine industry was a vehicle for circulating
these ideologies.

The changing social and cultural world brought about by urbanization and
industrialization also resulted in greater access to education and a more literate
population. Magazine publishers and advertisers wanted to reach this larger reading public. All of these social and cultural changes resulted in a shift away from
magazine content for the wealthy and a focus on subject matter for this growing
market of readers. The interest, though, was not in any reader but in women readers. Advertisers were most interested in reaching women who had become the
major household shoppers (Zuckerman 1998). Women made the decisions about
"wearing apparel, household furnishings and items of daily consumption" (Marzolf 1977, 207). Advertisers wanted a direct link to these consumers and women's
magazines proved the ideal platform. The cultural emphasize on women's domesticity by the late nineteenth century coupled with the desire to sell products to
women, resulted in women's magazines that were more focused than ever before
on the domestic sphere. All of these cultural shifts, which lead to the proliferation
of women's mass marketed magazines at the end of the nineteenth century, help
explain why women were increasingly being defined as consumers in American
society (Zuckerman 1998). Zuckerman explains, "These magazine aided in defining consumers of most goods as female and reinforced the message that to be
female was to be a consumer" (xv).

More than just constructing women as consumers, these magazines worked
to define standards of behavior for women of the time, instructing them on their

role in society, and more accurately, in the home as appropriate women, wives, and mothers. Then and now they can be described as "pervasive in the extent to which they act as agents of socialization, and the remarkable degree to which they deal in and promulgate values and attitudes" (Ferguson 1983). But many who have studied the history of women's magazines point out the variety of content available to women, including conflicting views, stereotypical portrayals, and positive representations (Endres and Lueck 1995; Walker 1998, 2000; Zuckerman 1998). The content has been described as sometimes leading in the presentation of women's lives, while at other times reflecting or lagging behind (Zuckerman 1998). Among the offerings in the late-nineteenth–century women's magazines were "columns advising readers about cleaning, cooking, making clothes, buying goods, supervising servants, and the home needs of husbands" (Zuckerman 1998, xiii). The content in these women's magazines during the first few years of the twentieth century included fiction and also some focus on topics related to the well-being of women and children (Kitch 2002). Stories highlighted issues related to child labor, tenement living conditions, education, and standards of public health (Kitch 2002). Throughout the decades content in American women's magazines has continued to change, indicating transformations in cultural values and interests throughout the years. Editors of women's magazines have occupied a powerful position setting "agendas of which topics are important or permissible, desirable or undesirable, worthy or not worthy of placing before the female sex" (Ferguson 1983, 10).

Many women's magazines started as pattern journals and offshoots of farm publications (Zuckerman 1998). For example the *Ladies' Home Journal* began as a column in a four-page agricultural weekly titled *The Tribune and Farmer*. The column addressed farmer's wives and was called "Women and Home" (Zuckerman 1998). Eventually the column became so popular that it turned into an entire section devoted to women and then, in December 1883, a supplement mailed out monthly. Other magazines grew out of the fashion industry, including *McCall's* (originally called *The Queen*), which advertised clothing patterns of tailor James McCall (Endres and Lueck 1995). The success of these women's magazines, and the numerous cultural changes that had taken place in the decades after the Civil War, inspired newspapers to target women readers.

Wanted: Women Readers

By the 1890s newspaper publishers, which often competed for advertising, knew they too needed to appeal to the women who were spending household incomes. And while other reasons may exist for why individual newspaper publishers wanted women to read their papers, the main goals in the newspaper industry were to sell advertising and to make money, not to inform and entertain women (Schudson 1978; Yang 1996). If newspapers appealed to women, newspapers would appeal to advertisers. Newspaper publishers had a problem, however.

While advanced education levels meant growing numbers of women were reading newspapers for the first time, women were not reading them at the same rate that men were (Abramson 1990). The reason, critics said: a lack of newspaper content addressing issues and topics of concern to women. The solution was to create pages specifically for women. Joseph Pulitzer is typically credited with the creation and popularization of these women's sections or pages though some conflicting accounts exist (Jordan 1938; Marzolf 1977). For example, in her autobiography Elizabeth Jordan writes of her first job editing a women's page at a Milwaukee newspaper in the 1880s (Jordan 1938). Pulitzer's *New York Daily World* began publishing columns in 1886 written by and devoted to women (Marzolf 1977). By 1891 the success of this target marketing strategy was evident—the one column had been transformed into an entire page carried in the Sunday *World* and devoted to women's fashion and society. The section continued to expand and by 1894, the *World* published at least one page daily "For and About Women" (Marzolf 1977). Jane Cunningham Croly (known as "Jennie June") is credited with overseeing these first women's pages (Kitch 2002). By 1896 William Randolph Hearst's *New York Evening Journal* had developed pages of women's content, as well, which reportedly tripled in size before year's end (Jackson 1993). Marie Manning, known for writing the first romance-advice column, edited the *Journal*'s section (Kitch 2002). The trend did not stop with the city's top two newspapers either. *The New York Freeman*, the country's leading African-American newspaper at the time, employed a prominent African American from Philadelphia—Gertrude Bustill Mossell—to write a "Women's Department" column (Kitch 2002; Streitmatter 1994).

The women's sections were not the only place, however, that publishers and editors placed content that might appeal to women. Toward the end of the nineteenth century, Joseph Pulitzer introduced new formulas for urban newspapers that caught on quickly and transformed the industry. The pages were now filled with colorful and sensational news, crusades, and elaborate promotions (Beasley and Gibbons 2003). Women were sent to cover murder trials from a "woman's" perspective and asked to perform stunts to gain attention and access to stories (Abramson 1990; Beasley and Gibbons 2003). From this era, two types of women journalists were born: "sob sisters" and "stunt girls." Sob sisters specialized "in tear-jerking accounts of flamboyant events" while "stunt girls" dressed up like beggars, feigned mental illness, and "posed as servants in the homes of society figures" (Beasley and Gibbons 2003, 64). The early part of the twentieth century marks the height of popularity for these kinds of female reporters (Collins 1980). Some of the most famous of these early women journalists are "Nellie Bly" (Elizabeth Cochrane), who raced around the world in seventy-two days, and "Annie Laurie" (Winifred Black Bonfils), who wrote tearful accounts of famous trials and exposés of social injustices. While these reporters were often intensely popular and appealed to both men and women, their reporting from a "woman's" angle was thought to especially interest women and draw them into the newspaper.

These examples of women's achievements beyond the women's sections of newspapers, however, are few. Most women working for newspapers at the end of the nineteenth century were expected to contribute to the newly developed gendered sections. That women began to have an established place of their own in the newspaper industry marks an interesting point in journalism history. Appealing to women readers as a means of marketing to advertisers was seen by editors and publishers at the time as essential but at the same time this strategy to separate "women's content" has had lasting effects on how editors consider gender in the construction of news content.

Food, Fashion, Family . . . and Feminism?

Women's magazines during the 1890s served as models for the newly developed women's pages. Publishers and editors placed topics understood to be of interest to women—fashion, food, family, health, etiquette, and homemaking—within these pages. The subject areas fell within a traditional notion of femininity—a sphere of domesticity—and highlighted the distinction between what has come to be known as feature news and the timely news found on the front pages of newspapers. This division of content forms the often heard "hard" and "soft" news distinction. Since the inception of women's pages and sections in U.S. newspapers they have published "soft" news content. They have told women what was fashionable, offered tips for self-improvement, called for community involvement, and advised women on their role as housewife and mother (Beasley and Gibbons 2003).

Historians, however, have noted that even if social events, fashion, and etiquette made up most of the content in women's sections, the pages offered women information on women's participation in public affairs, at universities, and world conferences (Marzolf 1977). These pages also at times offered feminist perspectives, though "it was dressed up in the latest fashions and accessories" (Beasley and Gibbons 2003, 142). The significance of these types of stories cannot be lost. While women's pages have been criticized since their inception for offering superficial content, they have continued to be a place where women's voices can be heard on a variety of topics of great importance. In fact, some of the most important stories of interest to women throughout the last century—the suffragist movement, birth control, and the pending nomination of the first female vice president—first appeared on the women's pages rather than front pages of U.S. newspapers (Marzolf 1977; Mills 1988). As Miller (1976) explains, traditional women's sections "offer more variety in their coverage than our memories give them credit for" (647). In the early 1900s, women's sections covered "the changing progress of women in jobs and professions and their demands for voting and other legal reforms" (Marzolf 1977, 207). As the century progressed, news about children's issues, health, rape law changes, domestic violence and women's wages could be found in these special sections (Lont 1995). An examination of women's pages over the years offers a glimpse at the cultural shifts, changing roles, and conflicting expectations of American women in the home and public sphere. For example, women's pages carried more content about women working outside the home after women were finally granted the right to vote and more young women attended college. Still, during this era content in these pages mostly considered homemaking issues and women's social roles while only occasionally the conflicts between work and home were covered (Marzolf 1977). This might be explained by the fact that during much of the life span of traditional women's pages most women that advertisers wanted to reach did not work outside the home.

Women's pages, along with the placement of women's news, also changed during World War II when women replaced men who had gone to war. During this time women moved into the work force, public life, and education, and occupied positions of power like never before (Lont 1995). Marzolf (1977) reports that in women's pages "day after day in the 1943 issues of the *Chicago Tribune,* for example, there were pictures of women pioneering new jobs in business, industry and in the military and earning the respect of society for their contribution to the war effort. Such columns as 'White Collar Girl' and 'Women who Work' ran alongside traditional columns with hints on cooking, fashion, beauty and social news" (209). Because women had some control over content in other sections of the paper, news concerning women moved onto front pages too. The literal move forward, however, did not last. As men returned from war and women returned to the home, women's news moved back to its own sections. Much of the content in women's section of that time mimicked the 1950s' idealization of wife and mother. Marzolf (1977) explains, "A look at the pages of the 1950s and early 1960s shows a return to the more conventional notion of woman as housewife and mother that predominated in those years of postwar peace. Although more women than ever were working, going to college and heading families, this fact went largely unnoticed in the women's pages" (209). But the changes in women's roles did not go completely unnoticed. Women's section editors continued to slip in serious content often without the notice or interest of upper management (Castleberry 1989). In fact, many women in newsrooms during the 1950s and beyond remember the women's movement and issues of importance to women—topics not making it onto the news pages—became common fare in women's pages across the country (Tuchman 1978). For example, stories about birth control, child abuse, and spousal abuse (Castleberry 1989; Marzolf 1977). One editor, Dorothy Jurney, described how in 1959 she volunteered to cover events and relieve her male colleagues and editors of work, as a strategy for successfully expanding the scope of her section (Streitmatter 1998). Mills (1988) notes the increasing trend in the 1950s to cover serious issues on the women's pages, explaining that a number of papers stretched the content in the women's pages "to better reflect women's lives. Giving them a political bite that men didn't notice because men didn't read them" (114). Talking about the *Dallas Times-Herald,* journalist Molly Ivins said reporters writing for the women's section when she started out " . . . got away with murder because dumb male editors never bothered to read it. . . . They were writing about birth control. Abortion. But it wasn't considered 'real news.' "(Mills 1988, 116).

While women's section editors most often receive credit for the progressive content on women's pages, male editors also identified the need to expand content beyond the stereotypical and traditional. Marzolf (1977) explains that a male editor at the *Miami Herald* asked women's editor Dorothy Jurney in the early 1950s to expand coverage in the pages to more closely illustrate women of the day. Along with the traditional content, the *Herald* published stories about equal rights for women, features on professional women, and Eleanor Roosevelt's column (Marzolf 1977). But during an interview later Jurney credited women in the newsroom, not her male editor, for the changes (Streitmatter 1998). Jurney said, "Back in the 1950s, male editors didn't give a whit what we 'girls' put in the women's section. Food, fashion, fluff—it was all filler to them. But some of us women editors thought differently; we wanted to start covering the substantive issues that women needed to know about" (Streitmatter 1998, 72). These editors employed a number of strategies to challenge the female stereotypes found on their pages. Marie Sauer, *The Post*'s women's pages editor from 1946 to 1968, used personal profiles about women in traditional male roles and "featured women's activities that were not considered feminine such as sports, politics, aviation, and adventures" (Yang 1996, 372).

Women's section editors were not only including content on contemporary issues, they were challenging the institutional traditions that went along with constructing these lighter news section. Women's section editors demanded a separation between advertising and their sections similar to what had been standard in the news department. Up until this time, women's sections were subject to the influence of commercial interests and often considered commercial in nature (Mills 1988; Yang 1996). The women's sections had been viewed in opposition to the serious tone of the news sections, "considered light and frivolous, with editorial content inextricably entwined with advertisers' and product publicists' agendas" (Beasley and Gibbons 2003, 141). Demanding change and respect in the newsroom, the women's section editors set guidelines that forbade reporters from accepting anything free offered by those on the outside and demanded their sections be printed in a more timely manner, which allowed them to carry timely news (Dishon 1997; Streitmatter 1998). Typically feature sections of newspapers had been (and many still are) printed days in advance of the news sections of the paper. This means that story deadlines are sometimes as much as a week or more before the stories are actually seen by readers. This advanced deadline created an impossible obstacle for reporting timely news.

The traditional coverage of weddings and other social events changed as well during the 1950s and 1960s. At the *Houston Post*, the editor took brides off the front page of the section (Mills 1988). Other women's section editors across the country followed *The Post*'s lead and moved brides off of their covers. Koky Dishon took over the women's pages at the *Columbus* [Ohio] *Dispatch* in the 1950s because she "had a vision of what they could be with coverage of real issues and writing that ignited the imagination" (Dishon 1997, 94). Later Dishon moved to the society editor post at the *Milwaukee* [Wisconsin] *Journal* where she did cover weddings. But she still broke from tradition. She explained how she was able to institute change: "Slide-rule editing, based on Old Family and wealth, governed the size of photos and stories for weddings. This changed when the daughter of a company president and the daughter of a factory worker in the same company exchanged vows in the same week. Their stories were paired equally, side-by-side, under one headline. The old formula was broken" (Dishon 1997, 95).

Women editing these special sections not only dealt with gender issues, but they also experienced and confronted rules and routines that reinforced racism. Dishon explained, "I started working when I was in my teens; when I grew up and looked around, I realized that I had never covered anything on the 'wrong side of the tracks' or been assigned to a black social event" (Dishon 1997, 96). Vivian Castleberry, the *Dallas Times Herald* women's editor from 1957 to 1984, described how her philosophy ran counter to the racist and elitist views that dictated women's sections and newspapers of the time. In filling her pages, Castleberry believed society news meant more than just writing about social clubs. She explained, "Anything that people do that is of human interest is part of the social milieu that makes up the whole society" (Streitmatter 1998, 75). One of Castleberry's most important achievements as a newswoman may have come when she inspired changes in photo policies at the *Dallas Times Herald*. Prior to and during the 1960s, the *Times Herald* had a rule banning photographs of African Americans in any section of the paper. Castleberry attempted to place photos of black brides on her pages but repeatedly met resistance from her editors. Finally in February 1968, Castelberry's persistence paid off and, for the first time since the *Times Herald* had been founded seventy years earlier, African-American faces were published in the paper. Soon after photographs of African Americans began appearing in other sections of the paper (Streitmatter 1998). All of these examples illustrate that while traditional women's pages may have limited female journalists' opportunities, they also offered women ways to construct and define news and change policy in newsrooms.

An investigation into content in *The Washington Post*'s women's section between 1945 and 1960 reveals the mixed messages in women's sections of the past and how women's pages typically "positioned readers in the roles of wives and mothers through traditional service features designed to cultivate a sense of femininity closely identified with domestic responsibilities" (Yang 1998, 371). But content in *The Post*'s women's section also offered examples of women who were defying gender norms, allowing women readers an alternative to a dominant gender ideology that prescribed traditional roles as the norm. A comparison of content in *The Post*'s women's section during 1945, 1953, and 1960 illustrates broad changes in the women's sections over this fifteen-year period (Yang 1998).

Most significantly, from 1945 to 1952, society stories dropped from 39 percent of stories to 13 percent, though by 1960 they were back up to 22 percent. Stories about clubs also saw a decrease, from 19 percent of the content in 1945 to 8 percent in 1952 and 9 percent in 1960. But while these traditional topics decreased, homemaking stories jumped from 1 percent in 1945 to 16 percent in both 1952 and 1960. This increase illustrates the heightened interest in women's roles in the home that were idealized during this era. Content about beauty was nonexistent in 1945, jumped to 9 percent of the stories in 1952, and back down to only 1 percent in 1960. Food, commentaries, fashion, and profiles all increased over the years (Yang 1996). Yang (1996) argues that the "comparison of the pages in 1952 and 1960 highlights Sauer's efforts to broaden the horizon of women's pages, despite social, and professional constraints" (371). When interviewed years after her career ended, Sauer discussed the professional constraints she encountered that prevented her individual agency in the newsroom. She pointed to management's preference for traditional women's section content dedicated to domestic concerns that, to a certain degree, were out of touch with women's lives (Yang 1996). Sauer also noted how advertisers played a role in how *The Post*'s management conceptualized its women's section. Sauer lobbied for a gender-neutral section in 1952 only to be turned down by her editors who later, in 1969, introduced a non-sex–specific lifestyle section. *The Post*'s management originally chose to keep women's pages against Sauer's wishes to satisfy advertisers' desires, illustrating the influence advertisers had on the women's pages (Yang 1996). Yang explained: "In order to pitch advertising toward affluent suburban housewives in the Washington metropolitan area, advertisers, preferring a traditional format focusing on women's activities, perpetuated the section's emphasis on women's domestic concerns" (Yang 1996, 368). This account by Sauer provides an illustration of how, decades after originally influencing how newspapers constructed women readers, advertisers continued to influence the topics and presentation of newspaper content. Yang (1996) explains, "In 1952, when Sauer proposed to transform the women's section, . . . a unisex section would have dispersed the concentration of female readers. To the management, a women's section following the traditional format appeared to be the best way to ensure a definite grasp of a mass of female readers" (368).

Women in the Newsroom

Women's absence in decision-making positions in the newsroom and, in turn, their limited access to define news and construct newspapers has been a problem dating back to the earliest newspapers and is seen as a contributing factor in what critics call the marginalization of content deemed important to women. During the early history of the newspaper industry, women rarely edited and/or published newspapers (Beasley and Gibbons 2003). When women did hold these decision-making posts, they had typically followed their husbands or families into the industry. In other words, they had inherited the position upon the death of a husband or father and performed the task out of necessity (Belford 1986; Kitch 2002; Schlipp and Murphy 1983). Toward the end of the nineteenth century women reporters became more common. But this occurred only when advertising became essential to newspapers' existence. At that point women were "actively sought as journalists to produce articles that would directly appeal to women readers and around which lucrative advertisements targeting women consumers could be placed" (Chambers et al. 2004). Newspaper editors often hired only one woman and they typically placed them in separate offices from male reporters (Beasley and Gibbons 2003). United States census figures illustrate the low number of female journalists in the early history of the industry. For example, only 288 of 21,849 journalists were women in 1880, which is less than 2 percent (Steiner 1997). The suffrage movement, however, helped to improve the status of women's news and women reporters and throughout the decades women saw a growth in opportunities in newsrooms across the country (Beasley and Gibbons 2003). The increasing numbers of women unfortunately did little to improve their status. Women reporters continued to be marginalized and segregated, expected to write from a feminine perspective and produce content for a female audience, while only a few made it onto the front pages where they were able to cover news in the traditional and straightforward manner of their male colleagues (Cairns 2003). Finally in 1915 the *New York Tribune* integrated women reporters into the city newsroom (Marzolf 1977). Another important time occurred in Washington in the 1930s when First Lady Eleanor Roosevelt mandated that only women were allowed to cover her news conferences (Marzolf 1977). This consequently meant more political reporting and "hard" news positions for women reporters. Women also moved into newsrooms in greater numbers during World War II. Marzolf (1977) notes that "by 1943 women made up 50 percent of the staffs of many newspapers in small cities and this trend was expected to continue," (69). However, this proved a short-lived gain as men returned from service and many women abandoned their posts in the newsroom—some willingly and some not. Those who did stay were typically moved back to their traditional beats, covering family, home, education, health, and welfare, writing features, and editing women's pages.

Opportunities for women continued in all areas of the workforce when between 1940 and 1960 the number of women working outside of the home doubled. During this time the numbers of women in newsrooms and media industry jobs grew as well. For example, the number of women editors and reporters working in the newspaper, magazine, and book publishing industries had increased by 7 percent during the 1940s (Marzolf 1977). The increase, though slow, continued through the 1950s and by 1960 women held 36 percent of all of these jobs (Marzolf 1977). Most often, though, women were reporters and more rarely did they hold editorial positions of power. And women of color were not afforded the same opportunities as white women. While black women journalists could be found reporting for black weekly newspapers, they rarely worked for the established mainstream press (Streitmatter 1998). The riots and civil rights protests of the late 1960s, however, compelled newspapers to finally start hiring more African Americans (Mills 1988). Other women of color prior to the 1960s, including Latinas and Asian Americans, were virtually absent from U.S. newsrooms.

This chapter has looked at the history of women's pages in U.S. newspapers from their introduction in the 1890s through the 1950s and briefly noted women's place in and out of the newsroom during these decades. It is significant to understand how women have been constructed as consumers of news and the positions women have occupied in newsrooms as producers of content. It is this construction of women that has aided editors in their definition of women's news. The confines of dominant ideologies about women and femininity and the cultural forces of capitalism have influenced these positions. Capitalism led to a pursuit of women, which thereby increased the amount of women's content and also caused newspapers to hire more women. Most significant in this chapter is the understanding of how and why newspapers showed an interest in female readers during the last decades of the nineteenth century. A grasp of the social and cultural shifts brought about by industrialization and urbanization, and the narrative behind the birth of the modern day women's magazine, helps to contextualize and explain the newspaper industry's courting of women readers. It also illuminates the reasons behind the construction of news from a gendered perspective. This account offers a context from which to appreciate the following chapters. In the next chapter I turn my attention to the 1960s and 1970s, the termination of women's pages, and the birth of modern-day feature sections. The chapter offers a discourse analysis of trade journal articles published during the time to help understand how those in the industry, particularly journalists working on the traditional women's pages and those working on the new feature sections, viewed this transition.

Chapter 3
From Women's Pages to Style Pages

By the 1960s women in the newsroom were caught in a bind: appreciative of the space and opportunities that women's sections had offered them, but frustrated by their inability to move important content and their bylines onto the front pages where the most serious news had a permanent place (Mills 1988; Chambers et al. 2004). Across the nation, a growing number of women and some men working in newsrooms and reading newspapers began pointing out inherent problems with this gender-driven story placement (Lont 1995). They did not view as positive the fact that women's pages covered serious news of importance to women. Instead they argued that these sex-specific sections, which marginalized women's concerns, signified more than just content placement. Placing "women's issues" on special pages, these critics argued, not only spoke to editors' perceived importance of the issues found there, but it also diminished the worth of the stories by indicating they were meant only for women and were of no concern to men (Yang 1996). Those opposed to special women's sections described them as "ghettoizing" women's content and serving as a "dumping ground" for any content marginally related to women (Lont 1995). Women editing and reporting for them were caught in a bind (Greenwald 1999).

Newspaper executives responded to the criticism and the modern-day feature section was born. According to Mills (1988), by the late 1960s *The Washington Post*'s editor had become dissatisfied with the "For and About Women" section. Mills explains, "He realized that a separate section for women implied that other sections were for men and not women, and was an anachronism in the modern world" (119). *The Washington Post*, which in January 1969 unveiled "Style," is typically credited with initiating the industry-wide move away from traditional women's pages (Yang 1996). Dishon (1997) says *The Washington Post* "did more to propel lifestyle sections into their golden era of the '70s and '80s than any other newspaper" by popularizing stories that showed the human dimension of hard news and used literary journalism to profile well-known people (99). Mills (1988) points out that the *Los Angeles Times* planned a similar transformation of its women's pages in the late 1960s, even though the paper did not debut "View" until July 1970. In September 1971, *The New York Times* changed the page one index to read "family/style" instead of "women's news" and altered the logo on the women's section to read "Family, Food, Fashions, Furnishings" rather than "Food, Fashion, Family, Furnishings" (Greenwald 1999). While some newspapers made this transition to style pages swiftly, others took their time. Eventually *The New York Times'* approach to style pages set itself apart from *The Washington Post* and *Los Angeles Times* in that it developed five thematic sections to replace its women's section, one for each day of the week (Mills 1988). A "Living" and a "Home" section were among the five sections and were looked at as replacements for the women's pages, indicating that the change may have had less to do with altering traditional constructions of the female newspaper reader and more to do with restyling the newspaper.

Many women, however, had expectations for these new style sections. With the transition came the idea that newspaper editors would show a respect for "women as readers and participants in the world, even its seamier side" (Dishon 1997, 98). Not only content, but also attitudes changed significantly, according to Dishon. She quotes a male executive editor of Long Island, New York's, *Newsday*, as saying, "I feel that women's pages should be a thing of the past. They were frivolous, nonsubstantial, and insulting to women" (Dishon 1997, 98). Newsday's new feature section was called "Part II." Dishon also quotes a *Chicago Tribune* Sunday editor as saying, at about the same time, "We decided a few years ago that women were interested in the same things as men" (98). An examination of the J.C. Penney-University of Missouri Awards program, which in 1960 began recognizing and promoting "the field of women's interest journalism," also illustrates changes in attitudes toward excellence of outstanding journalistic content in the area of human-interest news (Penney-Missouri Awards 1970, 2). By 1970 the women's and style pages were lauded as looking into "politics, the professions, voting, sex, drugs, religion and health. Not in textbook or lecture language but in timely, relevant description of local community activities and news events" (Penney-Missouri Awards 1970, 2). A study of newspapers noted for excellence by the J.C. Penney-University of Missouri Awards program from 1960 to 1971 indicates the progressive nature of the content (Voss, 2006). Marzolf (1977) points to the 1973 and 1974 awards to illustrate the trend toward less "fluff" and more substantive articles. While traditional topics continued to receive coverage, the nature of that coverage had transformed. She explains: "Staff writers reported in depth about the cost, quality and economics of food and they also wrote abut (sic) nutrition and health and truth in packaging, . . . Fashion writers covered the new fashion trends and consumer stories about fabric quality, safety and prices. In recognition of this trend, the Penney Awards for 1974 added a new category: consumer reporting" (Marzolf 1977, 203). Debate about the lines drawn between news and women's/ lifestyle pages continued through the mid-1970s. There seems to have been a lack of consensus in approaches to these sections, whether named for women or not, though most indications point to a concern with covering serious topics. Regardless of the approach, women's sections and the newly named style pages were earning respect. In 1976 the *Chicago Tribune* began publishing Tempo, known for its storytelling with a hard news edge (Dishon 1997). When Tempo writers won a Pulitzer Prize, it was official—feature sections had gained respect.

Times Were Changing

The discussions and changes going on within newsrooms were indicative of the times. Examining women's place in the newspaper mimicked a broader examination of women's place in society. The 1960s and early 1970s mark a time of heightened feminist activism and the women's liberation movement, a time that signified a shift in the status of American women. This cultural climate of radical social movements set the stage for changes in the newspaper industry and its construction of women readers. Among some of the largest cultural changes for women: more were graduating from college than ever before, they were marrying later, and with the introduction of birth control pills they were able to control reproduction like never before. While all careers were not entirely open to women, writing was considered an appropriate outlet so newsrooms became a suitable workplace for women. The presence of more women in newsrooms during this time was coupled with the existence of men whose attitudes also reflected a heightened awareness of the need for gender equality. The changing demographics in the newsroom and an ideological cultural shift likely affected publishers' and editors' construction of women readers.

In fact, a number of people—both within and outside of the industry—who have reflected on the elimination of explicitly named women's sections in the late 1960s point to second-wave feminism as setting the stage for changes in the newspaper industry and its construction of women readers. For example, Guenin (1975) wrote, "women's pages of American newspapers are changing, spurred by a variety of factors, not the least of which is the women's equality movement" (66). At the time women were rejecting the limitations of a family-centered role and pushing for equality in the workplace (Ryan 1992). Yang (1996) also makes note of the ideological changes outside of the news industry and the transformation within. She writes: "In the heyday of the women's movement, newspapers transformed the traditional women's pages into today's unisex lifestyle sections" (364). Marzolf (1977) explains: "In part these changes were in response to the issues raised by the women's liberation movement; in part these pages had been changing since the 1950s. In a receptive era of social change, some of the old stereotypes about women seemed hopelessly dated by the facts about women of the 1970s, and new names and fresh editorial approaches seemed appropriate" (199)

According to some reports, in calling for change, many women working in newsrooms at the time envisioned new sections that would take a human-interest perspective while news about women and "women's issues" would be integrated into all areas of the newspaper. Ellen Goodman (1993), a columnist for the *Boston Globe*, offers a firsthand account of her experience. She explained, "In the

1960s, these pages were the ghetto to which women, children, food, home and family were restricted. In the crest of the women's movement, many of us in the business embarked on a movement to integrate the whole paper" (59).

The growing number of women journalists likely had an effect on attitudes in the industry. By 1960, the number of women working as editors and reporters in newspapers, magazines, and book publishing grew to 37 percent of the total (Beasley and Gibbons 2003). Not only were there more women in the workforce and newsrooms, these women were demanding equality. By the 1970s, female journalists were still not getting jobs and compensation equal to men so they turned to federal legislation and the court system. Throughout the 1970s and into the 1980s, women used the threat of the Equal Employment Opportunity Commission to settle grievances. And when that did not work, they turned to the courts. The biggest cases included those at the Associated Press, *The Washington Post*, and *The New York Times* (Beasley and Gibbons 2003). These key gender equality cases in the legal system likely also had an affect on newspaper editors' decisions to terminate explicitly named women's pages.

Marketing played a role in the news industry's decision as well. The elimination of women's sections was not simply a decision to do what was right for women but to do what made good business sense to newspapers. As Mills (1988) explains, newspapers turned to a new format in large part because they were attempting "to upgrade the content and increase the readership of what had at too many papers become dowdy—and let's face it, boring—women's sections" (118). She explicitly links the shift to economic concerns, explaining, "newspapers always need to sell ads, and appealing to readers, not offending them, sells ads" (Mills 1988, 110). Within this context, it is fair to posit that newspaper editors did not transform these sections necessarily to reach a broader, non-gendered readership (i.e., males) but an extended female readership. In other words, they were altered in an attempt to create newspapers that appealed to those women fighting against the limited notion of wife, homemaker, and mother.

Types of Changes

Many of the newspapers that had not yet abandoned women's section by 1970 were significantly and rapidly changing the way they thought of them. The University of Chicago's Center for Policy Study surveyed seven-hundred women's page editors nationwide in 1970 and found that "a growing number of women [editors] are modifying and abandoning some of their traditional practices, with a new thrust toward more news and features which are genuinely relevant to the needs and interests of readers" (*Editor & Publisher* 1971, 9). Marzolf (1977) lists three approaches editors took at the time as they searched for a new identity to women's pages. The first, in the manner of *The Washington Post* and *Los Angeles Times*, was to rethink and rename the sections to reflect a wide range of interests to a diverse group of readers. A second approach, which Marzolf (1977) notes as more typical, was to implement new and expanded content while retaining all of the standard features of the former women's sections. A third method, typically chosen by small-town weekly and daily papers, was to keep women's sections as they had been until editors had evaluated how successful the first two approaches were at other newspapers. Dishon (1997) simplifies the approaches, offering only two categories. She explains, "There was still a division between two kinds of women's sections in the late 1960s. One embraced the so-called American dream, à la Ozzie and Harriet; the other perceived its readers as part of the real world" (97). A paper's circulation size typically correlated with the approach. Newspapers in small towns, with fewer people and a sense that readers know one another, remained more traditional. In bigger cities, where the news of a marriage held less significance to most of the population, newspaper editors rid their sections of that kind of content (Scott 1974).

What Really Changed?

Though the names of these pages changed, the new lifestyle sections continued to be thought of and often referred to as "women's pages." One reason for this was that many of the sections still included content thought to be of primary interest to women. Further, critics argued, advertising in the new feature sections continued to target women. Van Gelder (1974) noted: "The name may liberate the content but the section is still a dumping ground for anything male editors consider a 'woman's' story. So we get all the serious news about Equal Rights Amendments, rape-law changes, back-pay lawsuits, and so forth, back among the girdle ads instead of page one or two or three where they belong" (112). The varied degree of change may be attributed to the fact that not all in the industry agreed with abandoning women's pages and because of this a wide variety of approaches and philosophies prevailed through the 1970s. Media and feminist scholars, along with reporters, editors, newspaper industry leaders, and female audiences, asked critical questions about the transformation of women's sections. How the content of these newly conceptualized lifestyle pages changed—and whether or not the transformation away from traditional women's sections was good for women— became a topic of debate immediately. Many expressed concern that by creating sections targeting all readers, women lost out both in terms of content provided to readers and also the number of assignments and editorial positions for women in the newsroom. In other words, reducing traditional women's content did not guarantee more progressive coverage. In fact Marzolf (1993) noted the failure with mainstreaming news of interest to women. A further complaint launched at the new sections was that they had lost focus.

Exploring the Content: What's in a Name?

A few studies offer details about the content of women's pages and feature sections during these years of transition. Miller (1976) offers an analysis of content in 1965 women's sections and 1975 lifestyle sections, to illustrate how the content changed (or did not) in these renamed sections. She sampled stories, advertisements, and photographs during four separate weeks in 1965 and 1975 in *The New York Times, Washington Post, Chicago Tribune,* and *Los Angeles Times.* Miller categorizes the content into eight areas: lifestyle, consumer, food, fashion, social, entertainment/arts, syndicated features, and politics. After examining each of the newspapers, Miller noted that each of the newly named sections (with the exception of *The New York Times*) had decreased in size and all four newspapers had expanded their entertainment sections. Further, she found that except for *The New York Times,* which substantially increased the amount of lifestyle (including relationships and child rearing stories) and consumer coverage, style editors most often replaced traditional content with entertainment related stories. Miller also noted that within the lifestyle category, child rearing and activities for children had decreased the most. Further, she found that "despite their differing emphases on various topics, all four papers overwhelmingly focused on activities involving both men and women" (Miller 1976, 645). This fact seemed virtually unchanged from 1965 when the sections were designated for women. Finally, at all but *The Washington Post,* photographs of women dominated the new sections and roughly half of the advertisements were directed at women. Miller expressed concern that while in these newly named sections the content may address areas of interest for both men and women, advertisements most often addressed women and women primarily occupied the photos. She wrote, "If the first thing a male reader sees are photos of women and ads for women, he may not stick around long enough to examine the content and tone of the stories" (Miller 1976, 646). These findings help explain why many readers and journalists continued to (and often still) think of lifestyle sections as women's pages with stories that are of no concern to men. Miller concluded, "there have been certain changes in lifestyle sections since 1965. But, at some papers, there has been more talk than change. And, in some instances, the changes have been for the worse" (647).

Guenin (1975) had similar conclusions to Miller. She hypothesized that newly named and redesigned lifestyle pages would offer more relevant content to a wider variety of readers than did the traditional women's pages. She assessed content during April 1973 in six newspapers, three with new general interest style sections (the *Los Angeles Times, St. Petersburg* [Florida] *Times,* and *Davenport* [Iowa] *Times-Democrat*) and three newspapers with traditional women's pages (the *Philadelphia Bulletin,* [Phoenix] *Arizona Republic,* and *Albuquerque Journal*). The author analyzed content using a column inch count and designated categories using topics found in articles describing the transition of women's pages from their traditional format to general interest sections. Two categories were developed, "traditional" and "suggested." Suggested content included stories that had been had been determined to be desirable in the new sections, for example, community improvement and environmental stories, along with stories related to economics. Guenin's suggested content category included a long list of topics, including, "adolescence, aging, children, community improvement (including environmental stories), consumerism, economics, editorials and letters, education, employment, equality movement, family hobbies, housing, humor, legal problems, marriage, medicine, mental health, minority news, population control, single life, transportation, volunteer services and working women" (67). Guenin found that traditional content—advice, astrology, beauty, brides, fashion, food, home, and society—continued to take a large percentage of the space in the traditionally named sections while entertainment stories replaced traditional content in the updated style pages. Further her research illustrated that the updated sections fail to offer the types of suggested content critics hoped for (69). She wrote, "Rather than enlarge coverage of subjects deemed important to readers, it appears that efforts to upgrade the pages have resulted instead in the replacement of traditional copy with stories about movies, books, theater, travel, arts, and entertainment" (Guenin 1975, 69). Guenin also noted that the traditional women's pages are much less problematic than critics contend. She explained, "the *Bulletin* and the *Republic*, cover topics other than the traditional at least as well as the upgraded sections and also have food feature content" (69).

What Were They Really Thinking?

The remaining sections of this chapter present an analysis of newspaper industry journals during this time of transition. The analysis of industry discourse within these publications provides details of how those working in the newspaper industry during this time viewed this transition. Based on the cultural and industry climate of the time, this chapter attempts to answer two specific questions. First, to what degree did those working in newsrooms perceive the change as a means of empowerment for women news producers and readers? After all, in theory, editors planned to integrate women reporters and women's content into all areas of the newspaper, indicating that women would be treated equally. The second question asks to what extent did news workers express a resistance to this change? In other words, were women in the newsroom skeptical of the change? And were they concerned that their jobs and power to shape content might shrink?

I chose to analyze material in newspaper trade journals, business-to-business publications focused on news industry developments and dilemmas for three main reasons. First, there is an authenticity in the information that is not spoiled by a personal recollection blurred by time. Second, the method is likely to offer more summaries of the discourse, as this is the nature of written material. Finally, publishers, editors, and reporters throughout the country read articles in trade journals and, arguably, this discourse has an effect on decisions made broadly within the industry.

To locate content for analysis, I searched through every edition from 1969 through 1975 of *Editor & Publisher*, *The Quill*, and *The Bulletin*. While not an exhaustive list of the trade journals available to publishers and journalists at the time, these three publications were selected because by 1969 each represented a well-established, widely distributed magazine for professional journalists. *Editor & Publisher*, the country's oldest journal covering the newspaper industry, first published in 1901. Produced by the Society of Professional Journalists, *The Quill* began publication in 1909. The American Society of Newspaper Editors, founded in 1922, publishes *The Bulletin* (Branson, 2002).

I narrowed the data to 1969 through 1975 because these years cover the initial transition by *The Washington Post* and the primary time when other major U.S. newspapers were undergoing this transformation. On each page, headlines, sub-heads, and the text were scanned, including on the letters to the editor page. Articles were chosen for analysis if any mention of women's pages, style pages, or content related specifically to women existed. Some of the discussion about this transformation I found embedded in articles that focused on newspaper changes in general.

To determine to what degree news workers welcomed the transition to the so-called gender-neutral sections as a means for empowering women, I looked for voices critical of the traditional women's pages or that praised the newly formed style pages. To determine the level of resistance to the transition, I also looked for voices critical of the new style sections. Within these areas, the goal was to identify themes related to this empowerment or resistance. Finally, I searched for other themes related to the termination of women's page to better understand the general discourse.

Uneven Interest

I analyzed seventy-two stories in the three publications (Table 1). While some focused on the topic other articles only mentioned the women's or style section briefly, but these were included in the analysis because they offered insight into how many newspapers still included women's sections or had renamed (and/or reconceptualized) them as style sections.

Table 1
Number of articles by year and publication

	1969	1970	1971	1972	1973	1974	1975	**Total**
Editor & Publisher	16	8	8	6	12	4	5	**59**
The Bulletin	2	1	0	2	0	1	1	**7**
The Quill	1	0	1	2	0	1	1	**6**
Total	**19**	**9**	**9**	**10**	**12**	**6**	**7**	**72**

Of the seventy-two articles during the seven-year period fifty-nine were published in *Editor & Publisher*, six in *The Quill*, and seven in *The Bulletin*. Alone these numbers give some indication of the industry, these particular trade publications, and women's status within both. From 1969 through 1975, women throughout the country were demanding equality and acknowledgment of women's roles and value outside of the home. How often these publications covered women's issues, and the movement to transform women's sections, indicates the level of importance given to the topic and to women in general.

Only forty-seven stories included a byline: twenty-one were men, twenty-five were women, and one was unknown. However, within these twenty-one stories by men, one male writer, Howard Taylor, penned eight in an *Editor & Publisher* design column. During fifteen months in 1969 and 1970, Taylor published eight columns that focused on women's pages. The number of design columns devoted to women's pages indicates the level of aesthetic importance placed on these sections. Two other female writers contributed more than one article, so that there were fourteen unique male authors and twenty-one female authors. While the writers' gender (when known) does not indicate a particular perspective, gender bias could play a role in the overall story of women and news as told by these publications. That is because during the time of analysis, men held decision-making positions in these publications, like the news industry in general of the time (and to an unconscionable degree even now). To a large degree, then, men decided the importance of stories and issues, so the number of articles published about women's issues and women's/style sections during this period offers some indication as to the level of importance male editors gave to them. Considering that *Editor & Publisher* publishes weekly, with dozens of articles each issue, and the other publications published either on a monthly or bimonthly basis, the number of articles that appeared seems rather small during the seven years of analysis. Particularly within the context of comments declaring this as the time when modern-day feature sections were born.

Twenty-four of these articles describe and quote from conferences and workshops where discussion about women's pages occurred; conferences attended by dozens of editors and reporters from across the country. Further, seven articles reported on journalism research, many that had surveyed those in the news industry. These thirty-one articles alone offer a relatively rich set for analyzing industry discourse related to the transformation of women's pages and how newspapers packaged content for women. Most of those quoted and surveyed in the articles were women, indicating that women dominated the discussion about these women's/style sections. This is no surprise considering that women were typically in charge of the content. Additionally, ten of the articles focused on awards and announcements, including when newspapers renamed and redesigned women's pages; one article fell under the "opinion" category; and the others were news or feature news stories related to women. Of the seventy-two articles analyzed, forty-two specifically addressed the content transformations of women's sections and/or the name change (while others only briefly mention these sections in other contexts).

Content Matters, Labels Don't

The articles analyzed for this study primarily offered the perspectives of women (and a few men) who edit and write for traditionally named women's pages and newly named style sections. Overwhelmingly the articles that discussed women's or style sections focused on the content of these sections and how it was changing or needed to change, with much less space devoted to debating the names of these sections. One article, dated October 17, 1970 and published in *Editor & Publisher*, offered a confusing report about research conducted by a journalism student at the University of Southwestern Louisiana, Lafayette. Without much detail about the researcher's methods, the article reports in six brief paragraphs that "personality pieces, syndicated advice columns, and fashion news are favorite reading matter for women, according to results of a study of six women's sections" (*Editor & Publisher* 1970, 13). Further, the article reported that the author of the research "polled 20 women's news editors to learn which women's departments ranked highest in the opinion of the editors" (*Editor & Publisher* 1970, 13). *The Washington Post* and *Los Angeles Times* are included on the list even though by the publication date of the article each of these papers had officially terminated the women's pages in favor of a "style" section.

In another article *Washington Post* columnist Nicholas Von Hoffman discussed newsroom issues related to the women's section at his paper (*Editor & Publisher* 1971). Von Hoffman's remarks came after *The Post* had terminated the explicitly named women's section in 1969 and debuted "Style." These examples indicate that in the industry and in-house these style sections were still thought to be "women's sections." These examples are among many in the articles in which a newspaper's section, whether it was a new "style" or traditional "women's" section, was still called a women's section. It is clear through this analysis that these new sections were still thought within the industry to be primarily "women's" sections and the name change indicated little change in how these sections were perceived. Further, most of the articles that focus on women's or style sections detail the future direction of "women's news" content and the importance of featuring serious content with no voice advocating the elimination of explicitly named women's pages. Consensus within the discourse seemed to be that women's or style sections were needed because it was one place that women's voices and issues of interest to women could be located.

In 1971, six articles focused on the content of women's or style pages appeared in the trade journals. One, titled "How they would liberate the women's pages from drab content," summarized a conference in Chicago, organized by the University of Chicago's Center for Policy Study and the Urban Journalism Fellowship Program of the university. The extensive article, covering nearly three pages, describes the conversation of four (male) panelists and forty "women's editors" from the United States and Canada. One of these male panelists was Nicholas Von Hoffman, a columnist for the "women's section" of *The Washington Post*, though the "style" section had launched two years prior to the conference. The article explains that the conference was designed to "bring women editors together" and expose them to some important urban problems (*Editor & Publisher* 1971, 9).

But according to the article, most of the conversation addressed the remarks of Colleen (Koky) Dishon, editor and president of Features and News, Chicago, and former women's editor of the *Chicago Daily News* and *Milwaukee Sentinel*. Dishon said, "women's editors have made only small inroads into the business of covering and communicating 'real issues to women' " (*Editor & Publisher* 1971, 9). She complained that women's pages were "still glued to the old agendas" and that fashion coverage needed to take up less space. Dishon went on to argue that women's section editors needed to fill their pages with content addressing "the problems which many women workers have, including those with labor unions, management and schools" (*Editor & Publisher* 1971, 9). Rather than blaming women editors for the problems with these sections, Dishon and other conference participants pointed to male editors who were unwilling to allow change. The article explained that Dishon said she believed: "Women's editors find themselves trapped by a system that may at one time have served them well but is no longer flexible enough to let them do an adequate job of newspapering. It is clear, she continued, that men who control the newspapers are not ready to make the decision to change their women's pages" (*Editor & Publisher* 1971, 9)

In September 1971, *Editor & Publisher* published an article titled "Less chronicle, more guide: women's page style changed." The article, just a little more than a page in length, describes syndicated content for women's pages. The article both describes the editor of the new "Page-in-a-Package" and also the staff, providing insight into the type of content one could expect to find in the newly developed product. Editor Louise Hickman Lione's background, though primarily in fashion, also includes a stint as a feature writer. Stories about cooking, fashion, government and politics, "life-style," money and time management, crafts, and society "from the black writer's point of view" are said to make up the page's content. The article also states that in talking with editors about the page, Lione found that between 30 and 40 percent said they were "thinking seriously about changing the look and content of their women's pages by the end of the year" (Williamson 1971, 43). This insight offers an indication that the movement to reconfigure women's pages had taken off. Again, however, the names of the section and target audience were not the issue but rather the section's content and appearance.

An article titled "Editors: Don't drop women from paper's women's pages" and published in *Editor & Publisher* in July 1972, offers another example of the ongoing theme that the real issue is content and not a section's name nor the gender of its audience. The lead paragraph explains: "Changing the title of women's pages is not the answer to upgrading, not if the content remains the same" (Kelly

1972, 30). The article, more than two full pages, describes a "Women's Pages in the '70s" seminar held at the University of Kentucky at Lexington. At the seminar, sponsored by Southern Newspaper Publishers Association Foundation and Robert Murphy, the university's School of Communication's chair, editors warned that changing the title of women's sections is an all-too-common practice but is not enough (Kelly 1972). Conference participants pointed out that newly named feature sections directed at no one in particular were not the answer either. Forty-one people attended the three-day seminar—thirty-seven women and three men who held posts as women's editors and a male managing editor. According to the article, Murphy opened the seminar by suggesting, "perhaps there is no need for women's pages in newspapers; that such segregation is archaic" (Kelly 1972, 30). But the publication goes on: "He got no takers on his idea. Perhaps the most definite conclusion that came from the three-day seminar was that women's pages are needed, here to stay, and, for the most, getting better" (Kelly 1972, 30). Rather than terminate women's pages, seminar attendees agreed that women's sections needed to focus on the issues and problems relevant to working women since 49 percent of American women between eighteen and sixty-four worked outside of the home.

Participant Dorothy Jurney, women's editor of the *Detroit Free Press* in 1972, criticized the industry's move away from sections focusing on women. She said, "Some of the sections that have replaced the traditional women's sections in newspapers in America are not women's section in any sense of the word. They are feature sections and they have lost a great deal in change" (Kelly 1972, 30). The article continues to describe Jurney's perspective for approximately one-fourth of the story. It explains that Jurney said the elimination of women's pages was problematic because women lived different lives than men and desired distinct content in their newspapers. She said, "Women have a lifestyle that is different from men. They are still generally responsible for family, food and interpersonal relationships" (30). Jurney believed women should have a section of the newspaper where they can find these topics. But Jurney agreed with other participants that serious news stories in women's sections beat feature stories anytime. Jurney's point echoed the convictions of other participants; that women's sections belonged in the newspaper but that they should include stories of substance. For example, rather than provide a recipe, critics of the traditional method suggested writing about food industry safety. Another editor at the conference said, "I'm afraid that women's pages are relying on yesterday's subjects for today's pages" (Kelly 1972, 34). The editor called for "telling women new types of information such as how to run for office, where to get help with legal problems or even how hippie parents view childrearing" (Kelly 1972, 34). Participants blamed top management for not allowing women's sections to live up to this ideal.

Many articles offered evidence that content in these sections was changing and that the name changes indicated a renewed philosophical approach, even if it was still a gender-specific approach. Through her experience, Bea Anderson, editor of the "People" section in the *Orange Coast Daily Pilot*, illustrated not only changes in content but also how those changes were perceived. At the Palo Alto conference, she is quoted as saying:

> 'Last year we placed third in the Penney-Missouri awards,' said Bea. 'We had the club news, weddings and the usually [sic] trappings of the society pages, and I honestly felt we deserved no award. Then we completely redid our sections and called it "People." We began charging for weddings, just like we did for funerals. We threw out all club news unless the clubs were doing something special for the community. Surprisingly there were no complaints. We began doing depth stories: homosexuality, venereal disease, couples living together though not married—just a whole bag of things we never touched before. And I'm sure we brought more male readers to the section. This time we won first prize in the Penney-Missouri awards and this time I agreed we were entitled to it. (Scott 1974, 21)

Not all of the editors attending the conference with Anderson agreed on the specifics of women's sections, yet most agreed that "women's sections should be less social-minded; instead should enlarge their scope so as to attract male readers as well," according to the article (21).

By 1972, three years after *The Washington Post* initiated the move to "style" sections targeting both men and women, even outspoken feminist Gloria Steinem believed in the usefulness of a section for women. But her perspective is confusing (note her mention of men), and highlights a main problem of sections named for women: how do you define these sections and their content? Steinem is quoted as saying: "I've come back full circle in that I now feel the value of women's pages. They should cover all subjects, including men, from a point of view that is not being represented. There is a need for women's pages, but they should be more relevant than talking about subjects like turning artichokes into lampshades" (Long 1972, 37). This perspective, articulated by Steinem, highlights the complication between the content and the packaging of that content under a gendered heading. If a women's section includes men as its subject, what makes it a women's section? Further, what is it that makes content women's content? Is it the tone of the writing? Is it the reporter's gender? Is it the topic or how that topic is covered? Overwhelmingly during these early years of transition, editors and reporters discussed the content within these sections more than what to call them. And in these discussions they conceptualized the audience for these sections not so much as expanding to cover men but to cover a newly defined woman—one who works outside of the home and desires serious content versus homecare fluff. Consensus within the discourse indicated a call for serious content for and about women rather than the superficial. Nowhere within these trade journal articles, however, was there mention of the "ghettoizing" effect this could have on important "women's" issues.

Arguing for Integration

There were some voices, though very few, that believed the name of the section to be important, advocating for a general versus gendered term that would
indicate a new philosophy. These women wanted women's news integrated into
all sections of the newspaper. A three-page *Editor & Publisher* article, published
in April 1975, details that year's J.C. Penney-University of Missouri journalism
awards workshop. Seventy-five editors and writers attended, including nine men.
Debate at the conference addressed the "rigid vs. blurred lines between news and
women/lifestyle pages" (Williamson 1975, 30). The summary in the article indicates that by 1975 women's and lifestyle sections were essentially thought of as
interchangeable. Again, content was the focus of the debate and the name of the
sections took little space in the discussion. Much of the content discussion had
to do with what the article calls "old problems still being discussed" (Williamson
1975, 38). For example: how to deal with weddings on the women/lifestyle pages.
However, the article also hints at changed attitudes. Carol Sutton, the *Louisville
Courier-Journal*'s editor (and first woman managing editor of a major daily newspaper), is quoted in the article as crediting the women's movement with pushing newspapers to have a more "rational view of people and their society and,
therefore, of readers and their needs" (Williamson 1975, 38). She described the
philosophy at her newspaper: "We feel that women—both as readers and subjects
of news—belong all through the newspaper, on the front page, in the regional
news, in the sports section as well as in the features section" (Williamson 1975,
38). There is an indication that Sutton had moved beyond thinking of features
sections as women's sections. Her attitude likely represents others working in the
industry in 1975. But the article indicates that this integration Sutton speaks of is
not common practice at many papers. She is quoted as saying that she was "both
'surprised and a little disturbed' by a 'We-They' attitude expressed during seminar
meetings" (Williamson 1975, 38). The comments indicate that this integration
of content about women had not been fully realized at many newspapers, and
that whether named "women's pages" or something else, the feature sections of
newspapers continued to publish news for and about women. Another comment
by Sutton hints at the confusion within the industry. While addressing workshop
participants she said, "'I don't find many women's editors or people editors or
what-have-you editors . . . " (Williamson 1975, 38).

An article in *Editor & Publisher* published in July 1974 also spotlights a
changed attitude. The article, titled "Women's page changes noted by three editors," described a "Changing Women's Pages" session at the Editors' conference in Palo Alto, California. Elaine Levine, an executive editor of the Suburban
Newspaper Publications, Inc., that oversaw twelve weeklies in 1974, detailed how
traditional women's section topics were being turned into serious news stories.
She explained, "we like to tell [our readers] such things as where they can get
low-priced hamburger meat and where fruits and other commodities are not too
high" (Scott 1974, 21). Clearly, however, Levine does not describe any section in

her newspapers as a "women's section." The article quotes her as saying: "I don't know what I'm doing here for we have no women's pages in our paper" (Scott 1974, 21).

Sutton and Levine both represent editors who had essentially stopped calling their pages "women's" and had broadened the definition of their readers. Their perspective, found in later articles, indicates what seemed to be a minority but likely a growing trend. In these two articles, it was also evident that most of the section editors, even those who edited sections they considered to be women's sections, believed men should be part of their audience. This declaration again confuses the issue and begs the question: Why call it a women's section?

Resisting Change

Three articles highlighted explicit complaints about the industries' switch from women's pages to style sections and the move to publish more serious content. Two articles both published in 1972 offer a stronger perspective, urging editors to not drop women from the newspaper. One of these articles, titled "How much relevance can a woman take?" is especially interesting. In the two-page article published in *The Bulletin*, the author says women can read other sections of the paper for serious news and that the traditional content of women's sections should be saved. She compares the switch in women's/style sections in newspapers to the trend in women's magazines and explains: "I recently stopped buying *McCall's* with its glut of relevance—get rid of billboards and the shocking state of our water supply. Now I buy *Cosmopolitan* to find out how to drive men wild after my 40th birthday" (Roesgen 1972, 5). Throughout the article, the author also addresses issues of discrimination and says, "I think women's editors are in a stew over their own making, and their male bosses make handy scapegoats" (Roesgen 1972, 4). And later in the article she writes: "The best police reporter I know is a girl who looks sexy in a miniskirt, who dates a cop she really doesn't like just to get inside information and who knows when it's smart to act like a dumb blonde" (Roesgen 1972, 5).

An opinion piece published in *The Quill* in 1975 disagrees with the move away from women's pages and the lighter news found within them, calling for a mix of light and more serious or "relevant" news. The article begins by pointing to comments at the recent Penney-Missouri conference and also an article published in *Ms.* magazine. At the conference an Op-Ed editor for *The New York Times* told women's editors "to give the 'serious' subjects—abortion, child support, homosexuality and lesbianism—back to the city-side. She told them they had adopted a 'new Puritanism,' and were campaigning against 'homemaking, parties and fun'" (Lentz 1975, 29). The *Ms.* article, however, "applauds the 'serious' topics—abortion, rape, childcare and job discrimination on the women's pages" (Lentz 1975, 29). Lentz, the author of *The Quill* article, asks: "What's a women's editor to do?" Her article essentially acknowledges the schizophrenic nature of content in women's pages but, she argues, at least women's issues get "the best play" in these sections. Lentz's article is critical of the feminist argument for integrating women's news into all areas of the paper. Lentz (1975) writes: "When I hear the women's movement making noises because their news appears alongside of those other people, 'club women,' I wonder what kind of thinking process they go through. If it's women they are wishing to reach, is it the ones who have already been liberated beyond the women's pages?" (29). As for Lentz's title as a women's editor, she explains that she has tried other names but has only been successful in confusing people. In the end she seems to agree that no matter what the name, newspapers are infused with tradition and like it or not that means women's sections that will carry the food, fashion, and society news, along with "serious" stories for and about women. Other than in these articles, writers, editors, and reporters seemed to support the move to make content on women's pages relevant—regardless of the name of the section.

Calls for Equality and Respect

Another theme surfaced in the trade journal discourse and indicates a wider issue of gender discrimination during the time in the United States. Women editing these sections complained of discrimination against them and said the sections were held in low esteem. The problem, from the majority of those working on women's/style sections, was not in the name of their sections or the fact that issues of importance to women were segregated, but in resources and respect given to these sections and their editors and reporters. *Washington Post* columnist Von Hoffman complained, "we have editors and publishers who don't regard the (women's) section as part of journalism, but as an adjunct to the advertising department" (*Editor & Publisher* 1971, 10). This theme of treating women's or style section staff as second-class citizens and women's unequal pay and opportunities in the news industry came up in twenty-one articles. Two examples of this theme follow.

An October 17, 1970 *Editor & Publisher* article reported that at a conference "Several of the women editors volunteered that better women's sections could be produced if more newspapers would treat the women's staff as the equal of the cityside staff, hire women reporters as carefully as they hire newsroom reporters, pay them adequately and demand professional performances" (*Editor & Publisher* 1970, 13). A three-page article in *Editor & Publisher* in 1971 quotes a conference participant who criticizes the treatment of women's pages and indicates how widespread this bias spans within the industry. The article reads: "In most places, the women's page is low prestige. . . . If you doubt that, look at the rest of the newspaper, look at the sections they are interested in. Look at the contents of *Editor & Publisher*, their magazine, the publication that reflects their interest and their concerns about newspapering" (*Editor & Publisher* 1971, 10).

What Does It Mean?

Evidence found in the analysis indicates women working in the news industry did not care much about the changing names of these women's sections nor did they have a problem with the fact that newspapers had special sections targeting women. In fact, these sections were generally seen as important and needed. Very few voices expressed a desire to change the news industry's tradition of segregating "women's issues." Instead, the concern at the time focused on the content within these sections and the treatment of the staff working on these sections. Most of those contributing to this discourse wanted to offer relevant content to their readers—for example, consumer reporting on food women prepare for their families versus recipes for preparing that food. In fact, the discourse was dominated by concern with the type of content and not with the title above that content. Often even when the name of a section had changed, those working on it still referred to it as a "women's" section. One reason for this was that the newly named sections still included content thought to be of primary interest to women and also content that had been published in traditional women's pages. But this finding points to an obvious question: Why did the industry move to change the name of women's sections if in-house the sections remained the same in both theory and practice? After all, the content change had been occurring for years, according to those who had worked on women's pages in the 1950s and 1960s. One explanation could be that the name change was simply a strategy to ward off criticism and appease women and feminists. It could also have been a strategy for revamping an outdated section in order to gain readers and advertisers, but not necessarily male readers, newly defined women reader that advertisers were anxious to reach. It is likely that in the wide range of U.S. newspaper editors these motivations, along with the altruistic belief in integrating "women's content" into all sections of the paper, played a part in the industry's so-called transition to "style" pages. From the discourse within the trade journals, however, the change in these sections seemed to be more in theory than practice. After all, the discourse indicates, men in charge of newsrooms offered few resources to improve these sections.

The late 1960s and early 1970s can appear to be a progressive time when the industry reconsidered and restructured its female audience, with grand ideas of integrating women's content into all areas of the newspaper and offering less stereotypically gendered notions of "soft" news. This chapter, however, tells a different story. From the analysis it is clear that within newsrooms across the country, early on the transition from women's to style sections was little more than a name change, and certainly not an attitude change. In other words, this change did not significantly restructure how editors and reporters were thinking about these sex-specific sections. It seems to be a time when appearances changed, but within the newsroom women readers were still constructed in a limited way, particularly by male editors.

Women working on these women's (and style) sections within newsrooms were pushing for a broader definition of their readers and for more resources to deliver content they believed to be important to women. But the analysis indicates they were not in a hurry to get rid of sections targeting women. Maybe because of their experiences they knew all too well that the notion of integrating women's content would not work as long as male editors continued to hold sexist views of women both in and out of the newsroom. Maybe they did not want to lose the one place where they had the power to define news. After all, as women's pages turned into style pages more men began editing them.

Theoretically this transition marks a significant time in how newspapers constructed a female readership. What seems, however, to be most significant about this time is how insignificant the change really was within the news industry. The majority of those participating in this discussion, most of which were women, believed that women's and style sections were interchangeable. What they also believed was that these sections should publish stories about serious or "relevant" issues that affect both men and women. Still the "serious" topics named have traditionally been thought of as "women's issues," including abortion and childcare. Further, this call for serious stories was not a new concept. The change in women's sections was ongoing and had started much earlier than the movement to switch the names. Previous publications indicate that the movement to include serious content in the women's pages of newspapers began soon after the birth of these sections in the 1890s and had taken on momentum in the 1950s. What also had not changed was how editors and reporters of these sections were constrained by management, expected to cater to advertisers, and offered limited resources. Again, previous work on this subject indicates these complaints are nothing new. Women working on lifestyle sections in newsrooms during the 1970s were still struggling with the constraints that women working on "women's pages" had been encountering for decades.

These findings illustrate that the second-class status of women inside newsrooms and on the pages of newspapers was no different than in many other places within the public sphere. But contrary to what many might believe, many women in newsrooms during the 1970s were not fighting to rid their papers of women's sections. Instead they were developing and employing strategies that their newsroom sisters before them had used to produce relevant content for women. Women were caught in a sort of double bind, which helps to explain why they were not trying to fight the system. They believed women's sections were necessary because at least in these sections news of importance to women would get play and women would have opportunities to shape news content and ultimately construct reality.

This chapter reveals how women journalists were talking about women's pages, women's content, and women readers in 1969 and into the 1970s. Taken within the context of previous research examining the new style sections of the 1970s, this research is telling. Content analysis of the new style sections found they continued targeting women through advertising while expanding entertainment stories instead of including important suggested content (Guenin 1975;

Miller 1976). Together the research indicates that ultimately women journalists during the 1970s continued to have little power within the newsroom. Even so, like women throughout the country who were fighting for equality, women in newsrooms were talking and organizing and pushing for changes. What they were not talking about, however, was the problem with having a separate section for women readers. For all of the complaining found in the literature calling these sections a "dumping ground" for all things related to women, surprisingly this did not surface in the discourse. Apparently most of the women within the discussion found the idea of abolishing women's sections to be worse than the "ghettoization" of women's issues. Again, this could be explained by their belief that issues they felt were important to women would be absent from the newspaper if they as women's section editors and reporters were not writing about them and placing them in a section targeting women. Further, it is worth repeating, women working on these sections (largely because they were ignored by male editors) had the power to define news, and they can be credited with expanding traditional definitions of news.

While style pages have continued to have a place in U.S. newspapers, by the late 1980s the newspaper industry had become worried about a declining female readership. In general, newspapers were seeing a readership drop, but the decrease in women readers was at a higher rate than their male counterparts. Wanting to gain back women readers and attract advertisers, a number of newspapers again started producing explicitly named women's pages. The next part of the book details this transition back to explicitly named sex-specific pages and presents case studies of contemporary newsrooms. Through interviews with thirty-five journalists, the remaining chapters of the book detail how these contemporary women's pages have been conceptualized and constructed, along with how they are embraced and resisted in newsrooms.

Part III

Contemporary Women's Pages: Case Studies

Chapter 4
Same Problem, Same Solution

By the late 1980s the newspaper industry had seen a steep decline in its female readership. Motivated industry leaders decided they needed to get women back, buying and reading newspapers. After much consideration, many editors and publishers again considered the appropriateness of explicitly named women's sections. The solution was met with mixed reactions. Supporters argued contemporary women's sections would cover concerns of women readers that were neglected in the male-oriented news profession and that having a space for women's concerns was better than no space. Critics echoed the complaints of the past, calling contemporary women's pages a separatist and sexist solution that marginalizes women's concerns. This chapter explains how and why publishers, editors, and reporters at three newspapers—*Chicago Tribune, Lexington Herald-Leader* (Kentucky), and *Capital Times* (Madison, Wisconsin)—reintroduced explicitly named women's pages to their audiences. The case studies together offer a general understanding of how newspapers reevaluated and reconstructed women readers during a time when the industry paid particular attention to this demographic.

The industry-wide discussion to reintroduce women's pages came about as part of a larger dialogue focusing on newspapers' declining female readership, a matter that dominated industry conversation throughout the 1990s. The loss of women readers presented newspapers with the worry of losing valuable advertising dollars and was reminiscent of the interest in advertising to women within the industry during the 1890s. The number of articles on the topic appearing in newspapers and trade magazines in the early 1990s, along with industry research, indicates the intense interest given to the topic. Many of the articles make it clear that the reality of losing advertisers was driving the industry's interest in women readers. A 1992 *The Wall Street Journal* article explained, "Newspapers have good reason to be concerned about their female readership. Besides making up 52 percent of the population, women are far more likely than men to be making buying decisions" (Pearl 1992, B1). Further evidence of worries related to advertising is found in the Newspaper Advertising Bureau's interest in the topic. The group released a study showing that between 1970 and 1990 adult women daily newspaper readers dropped by 18 percent compared with a decline among male readers of 12.5 percent during that time (Hansen 1992). An article published in the *Wash-*

ington Journalism Review reported an even higher decline in female readership, explaining that the frequent readership (reading a paper four days out of five) of women declined by 23 percent between 1970 and 1990, while for male readers the decline ended at 16 percent (Braden 1991).[1] The Newspaper Advertising Bureau reported that between 1982 and 1987 women who were frequent readers actually dropped 26 percent (Stein 1990). According to a survey by Simmons Market Research Bureau, on a typical day in 1991, 60 percent of women read a newspaper compared to 67 percent exactly ten years earlier (Pearl 1992). A 1997 Media Usage Study reported "regular weekday readership of newspapers averaged 5 percentage points lower for women than men (49 percent versus 54 percent) among the three thousand adults interviewed for the nation-wide study" (Miller 1998). Additionally, industry research pointed out that the younger the reader, the greater the gap (Schmidt and Collins 1993). While the percentage point differences may seem relatively small, it translates into millions of readers. One report explains, "Had we maintained our appeal to women equal to what it was in 1970, we would have seventeen million more readers" (Knight-Ridder 1991, 8).

Theorizing the Loss of Female Readers

Along with a number of articles in industry magazines highlighting these statistics, a number of theories about the growing gender gap surfaced. Some reasoned that women working outside of the home had less time to read newspapers so naturally as more women left home for work, fewer women read newspapers. But studies showed women who worked outside of the home actually were more devoted to newspapers than women who stayed home (Hansen 1992). Another theory reasoned that women's longer life span explained the phenomenon. As one article noted, "readership declines as people age, . . . making women—who generally outlive men—seem like they're reading less" (Hansen 1992, 23). But the rise in circulation of women's magazines and the fact that women outpurchased men when it came to new books showed the weakness of this reasoning. A *Gallup/Publishers Weekly* poll reported that in 1993 women purchased 59 percent of all books, and a Magazine Publishers of America study found that working women rely on magazines for information more than any other medium (Kelly 1993).

Rather than point to a change in women to account for their readership decline, industry leaders began to focus on newspapers. Ultimately, many came to believe that the problem was not with women but with newspapers not offering women the content they desired. In 1992 Jennie Buckner, vice president for news at a Miami-based Knight-Ridder newspaper chain, was among the many to voice frustration over the fact that women were not represented in newspaper content (Pearl 1992). In fact, twenty years of research had documented the shortcomings of newspapers in covering women, topics of interest to women, and women's voices (Bridge 1995; Miller 1993; Tuchman et al. 1978). A 1991 survey of 154 women in seven cities detailed what women care about and want to read in their daily newspapers. The topics included children and their future; money and time; safety and health; success stories; workplace issues for women; ethical, moral, and social issues; family and personal relationships; personal fashion, home fashions; and hobbies and pastimes (Knight-Ridder 1991). Other research indicated women desired local community news, followed by advice columns and international news (Miller 1989). Professional sports topped men's list of favorite topics, followed by international news, and local school sports. Industry critics compare the topics men and women want to read with how newspapers allocate resources for those topics, and say it becomes clear why women do not find what they are looking for in a newspaper. Research has shown that two of the topics women read least—local sports and business—take up 27 percent of newsroom staffing (Miller 1989). Fashion, lifestyle, and food, which men rank amongst the least interesting, receive only about 8 percent of newsroom staffing. During the 1990s not only were there complaints that topics of particular interest to women were not appearing in newspapers, but also women were much less often used as sources in news stories and pictures of women—other than in fashion spreads—continued to be comparatively rare.

Research that had been done on the relatively new lifestyle sections indicated they had primarily become entertainment and light-hearted features sections. It seemed that in ridding newspapers of traditional women's sections, news copy about women and topics of interest to women had significantly decreased rather than having been mainstreamed as planned. In other words, the "mainstreaming" approach meant to incorporate news of interest to women into all sections of newspapers had not worked. Instead, content of particular concern to women and about women newsmakers had nearly disappeared (Bridge 1995).

Industry leaders and women in newsrooms suggested a number of ways to turn the gender gap around. Among them: include more women in decision-making positions in the newsroom; invite female reporters to budget meetings; restructure beats to cover issues rather than institutions; and rather than simply cover facts, report what those facts mean to people's lives (Hansen 1992; Kelly 1993; Miller 1989; Miller 1998; Schmidt and Collins 1993). But another more controversial solution—to reintroduce explicitly named women's sections—gained popularity. By the early 1990s a number of papers, including the *Chicago Tribune* (one of the largest metropolitan daily newspapers in the country), had introduced new women's sections. The *Tribune* debuted a weekly section called "Woman News," while the *Lexington Herald-Leader* (Kentucky) offered "YOU" with the subtitle "News for Today's Women." The *Arizona Republic*, the *Cleveland Plain Dealer*, the *Virginian-Pilot* (Norfolk), *Ledger-Star*, the *Corpus Christi Caller-Times* (Texas), and the *Portsmouth Herald* (New Hampshire) also introduced women's pages with names like "Woman Wise," "Women's Weekly," "For Women Only," and "Hampton Roads Woman" (Knight-Ridder 1991; Pearl 1992). From 1991 to 1992 one article estimated about ten newspapers revived women's pages (Hansen 1992). In a 1993 article, Nancy Woodhull, a former editor of *USA Today* and president of Gannett News Service at the time, estimated at least forty U.S. newspapers published explicitly named women's sections (Schmidt and Collins 1993).

Missing Content, Missing Women

The problem with how women have been both portrayed and left out of newspaper content has been well documented. The Women, Men and Media project, which began tracking newspaper coverage of and by women in 1989, examines front pages of major-market, general-interest newspapers in diverse geographical areas (Bridge 1995). On the front pages of these newspapers during January 1993, the stories referred to or solicited men for comment 85 percent of the time. Further, men wrote 66 percent of the front-page stories, and men appeared in 73 percent of the front-page photos (Bridge 1995).

Many critics argue that the missing content in U.S. newspapers is due to the lack of women in the newsroom, particularly in decision-making positions. In 1982 men held more than 90 percent of top editor jobs in the nation's newsrooms, according to *Editor & Publisher* yearbook listings (Jurney 1982). The percentage becomes even higher when only looking at newspapers with a 250,000 or higher circulation. An American Society of Newspaper Editors 1983 survey illustrated that in major U.S. newspapers there were ninety-three women editors and 1,027 men occupying the post, while sixteen women and 893 men were executive editors (Miller 1985). In other words, men occupied 89 percent of the top management positions. Minority women have even held less power in the newsroom. The American Society of Newspaper Editors reported in 1987 that while African Americans made up 3.62 percent of newspaper employees, Latino men and women constituted 1.68 percent of the workforce and Asian Americans made up less than 1 percent of the total (ASNE 1987). At the time, the report noted, minorities made up 20 percent of the population but only 6.56 percent of newsroom workers. But regardless of color, gender alone has been enough to keep women from becoming top editor and occupying other decision-making positions within a newsroom. Women throughout the 1990s made slow progress in acquiring decision-making positions in newsrooms across the country. Further when women have been named to top posts they too often continue to be relegated to positions within the "soft" news, features, and women's sections.

Statistics regarding the numbers of men and women in newsrooms and top editorial positions are especially interesting in the context of journalism education and make invalid the argument that competent women are unavailable. Between 1977 and 1985 about 60 percent of enrolled students in journalism and mass communication programs were women (Miller 1985). Together these statistics suggest that while capable women are available to fill editorial jobs, men most often attain the positions. A National Federation of Press Women report indicated women's progress had still not changed much by the early 1990s either. In 1992, Hansen reported women held about 10 percent of the editor and executive editor positions at papers with circulations greater than two-hundred-fifty thousand. In 1993, Mills reported that women accounted for 39 percent of the overall newspaper work force but that only about 18 percent of these women worked as news executives. At this time, Mills (1993) also noted "just 8.5 percent of newspaper publishers are women; 9.3 percent of editors in chief or executive editors; 12.6 percent of editors and 11.7 percent of editorial page editors" (25). A survey by the Freedom Forum in 1993 indicated that 34 percent of all journalists were women while a 1992 survey by the National Federation of Press Women showed women fill only 19 percent of newsrooms' top editorial and management positions (Schmidt and Collins 1993). Further, in 1993, women accounted for only 10 percent of the nine hundred members in the American Society of Newspaper Editors (Kelly 1993). And even with more women editors than ever before, industry insiders have continued to discuss the lack of women in senior management positions (Kelly 1993; Schmidt and Collins 1993).

Industry critics argue that the few women in newsrooms, and even fewer in decision-making positions, among a majority of men have served to intimidate and silence women. In other words, women have been forced to become "one of the boys" or face being singled out and viewed as difficult. Schmidt and Collins (1993) explained how this male-dominated ideology in newsrooms affects women. They explain: "At newspapers where most of the editors are men, budget meetings can turn the conference room into a locker room. Often, the editor who shouts the loudest is the one whose story makes it on page one. . . . Women editors who pitch women's stories risk being labeled the 'workplace mommy' or the 'workplace feminist,'" (Schmidt and Collins 1993, 42). Media critics during the late 1980s and the early 1990s argued that with so many men in decision-making positions it is no wonder much of newspaper content does not appeal to women. Men define news and, therefore, news is defined through a masculine value system—framed by conflict and authoritative figures within government and politics, the police, and courts. The argument is based on social beliefs about how biologically and culturally women and men experience life differently even in the 1990s. Among these differences, critics within the industry pointed to the fact that women are generally the primary caregivers and homemakers in a family unit and typically earn less money and face fewer political opportunities than men. These differences are believed to lead to distinctive sensibilities and interests and approaches to news. Industry articles indicate there was discussion at the time that newspapers were relying on the language of the establishment, conflict, and controversy and therefore newspaper editors and reporters were approaching their stories from a male-world viewpoint that is less appealing to women (Hansen 1992; Kelly 1993). The articles that discussed this perspective were addressing the concern over lost women readers and considering reasons for the loss and ways to bring women back to newspapers.

A "Godsend" or Contemporary "Ghetto"?

As newspapers reintroduced women's pages in the 1990s, the debate over whether to designate newspaper content according to sex or gender continued to be grounded on the same points as they had been decades earlier. While some argued the designation marginalized women's concerns, others said some space for women's concerns is better than no space. Depending on who was speaking, contemporary women's sections were an indication of tokenism or of progress. Supporters argued contemporary women's sections would cover concerns of women readers that are neglected in the male-oriented news profession. Critics called the solution separatist and sexist. The debate extends beyond the borders of the United States, too. In "The Women's Page: Godsend or Ghetto?" four media practitioners from around the world were asked a series of questions about women's sections. Their conversation exemplifies two main perspectives—for and against—reintroducing women's pages. Often the support comes from a sense that ghettoized news is better than no news. Anita Anand, director of Women's Feature Service in New Delhi, India, argued, "Until women can claim equality in the media, especially representation in significant numbers in decision-making positions, women will have to try to maximize all the spaces made available to them in the media" (Media and Gender Monitor 1998). Speaking against segregated news, Pat Made, the regional director of Inter Press Service in Africa, argued gendered sections "Wrongly give the impression that women can be separated from the rest of society" (Media and Gender Monitor 1998). In a separate article, American feminist writer Susan Faludi said, "The whole idea that women's news and issues are special or subordinate to men's is implicit in the creation of these sections" (Cox 1992, 8). Many women reporters are troubled by these new women's pages as well, explaining that regardless of their intention they "are inherently unequal. 'It's a silly way to label news,' says Anna Quindlen, the former deputy metropolitan editor for *The New York Times* and now its third woman columnist" (Kelly 1993, 35). A managing editor at the *Detroit Free Press* (who became vice president of news for Knight-Ridder) wrote in the 1991 Women Readers Task Force report, "Please don't tell me that in a gender-obsessed world, a women's section won't emphasize the perceived and demeaning differences that women are struggling to erase" (Knight-Ridder 1991, 6). Along with criticism launched from within the industry, a number of newspaper editors who have added women's pages have received angry letters and phone calls from female readers (Hansen 1992; Pearl 1992). Ultimately, critics of contemporary women's pages argue, even if the new pages have solved part of the readership problem, two main problems remain: an absence of women in content throughout most sections of the newspaper and an absence of women in decision-making positions within the industry.

The Chicago Tribune—Presenting "Woman News"

A telling indication of the newspaper industry's deep concern with losing women readers came when the American Society of Newspaper Editors (ASNE) spent $200,000 and two years to study disenfranchised readers (Hansen 1992). The Future of Newspapers committee, which oversaw the study, produced a prototype developed by Colleen (Koky) Dishon, associate editor of the *Chicago Tribune*, and titled "WOMENEWS" (Kelly 1992).[2] Dishon's participation in the project may seem ironic in light of the fact that upon joining the *Tribune* in the mid-1970s one of the first things she did was "kill the ladies' pages" (Schmidt and Collins 1993, 40). The unveiling of "WOMENEWS" came in April 1990 at the annual ASNE convention. According to one description of the fourteen-page prototype, it included in-depth coverage of women newsmakers, a story about a turning point in one woman's life, columns on relationships, parenting, and careers, and a classified advertisements page for services such as baby-sitting, child care, fitness, and children's parties (Hawley 1997). Dishon said to create "WOMENEWS" she borrowed ideas from women's magazines and then presented them in a local context (Braden 1991). The *Tribune* also conducted focus groups with Chicago-area women who showed "unanimous condemnation" prior to seeing the "WOMENEWS" prototype (Kelly 1992). After examining the newly formed women's pages, however, readers showed enthusiasm. One account explains: "They were changed women. This is really good, they were saying. This is news I can use. This speaks to ME!" (Kelly 1992, 12). Soon after presenting ASNE convention attendees with the prototype, the *Tribune* launched a Sunday section titled "Woman News." The *Tribune*, however, had actually reached out to its female audience a few years prior with "Tempo Woman" but the newer "Woman News" section targeted a younger and hipper audience than its predecessor (Hansen 1992). "Tempo Woman" had existed since the mid-1980s. Hawley (1997) explains it began when *Tribune* research first warned of a steep decline in readership among women. In response, Marjorie David, then an assistant editor of the Lifestyle section, created Tempo Woman. Several regular "Tempo Woman" features were carried over to "Woman News," which was the name of "Tempo Woman's" standing head for news briefs. Denise Joyce, who in 2002 edited a weekly health and family section at the *Tribune*, served as Lifestyle editor during the launch of "Woman News" and supervised the project. She described "Tempo Woman" as much more of a traditional feature section.

According to an early study on readers of "Woman News," the section successfully appealed to its target audience. The report explains: "71 percent of readers who were aware of the section said they found it appealing. Among eighteen- to forty-year-olds, the appeal was more than 80 percent" (Hansen 1992, 25). Through additional focus group research, the *Tribune* found that a large number of men also read the section (Miller 1998). Dishon and others attributed the success of "Woman News" to the fact that the pages produced for and by women offered women the opportunity to see themselves in the paper (Stein 1990). Advancements in fertility treatments and the trials of a lesbian minister were among the stories during the first year of "Woman News" (Hansen 1992). While some argue that the gender of journalists does not affect news, these comments by women in the *Tribune* newsroom indicate a belief that women journalists do affect content and readership. Another woman reporter's remarks at the *Tribune* in 1992 offer further evidence of this belief. She said that "Woman News" published "thought-provoking stories that wouldn't have gotten into the paper anywhere else" (Hansen 1992, 25). In 1998, "Woman News" editor Marla Krause, also echoed the point. She explained, "We bring stories that would never be in the paper otherwise: childcare, women's health, women's issues. If not for us, women in the workplace and domestic violence would be only breaking news. We bring a well-rounded view of women" (Miller 1998, 42).

In my discussion in 2002 with Geoff Brown, one of the *Tribune*'s associate managing editors of features, Janet Franz, editor of special sections, Denise Joyce, the health and family section editor, and Jean Rudolph, an editor for the *Tribune*'s magazine, they recalled their impressions of the "Woman News" launch and Dishon's motivations behind the project. They remember Dishon's concern that women were not finding themselves on the pages of the *Tribune*. Dishon also believed that having women in decision-making positions alters content because women have different views on what is important. She explained: "A lot of what we did could have been done by other sections. . . . But they didn't do it" (Miller 1998, 42). Franz, associate managing editor of features during the development and launch of "Woman News," explained how the section presented women information on important topics. She said, "A lot of [Dishon's] thinking was always on top and intuitive and on the mark. And I think what she saw were all these feature sections folding, they were all dying off and I think her thinking was that now more than ever women needed that section where they could pull the news, one place where they could get the news of women's issues, feminism, and what was happening" (Franz 2002). Joyce, the lifestyle editor during the unveiling of "Woman News," and Brown, who served as the entertainment editor during the early 1990s, also indicated that the section began because with the elimination of traditional women's pages content for women had disappeared. Rudolph, the editor of "Woman News" for three years starting in 1999, offered evidence that at least some readers may have felt the same way. She said, "I was a big fan of 'Woman News' all my life. Since it started I read it as a reader before I worked at the *Tribune*. One thing I always thought was that there were things in here that wouldn't be in any other section. There are lots of stories that would or could be" (Rudolph 2002).

While accounts from Dishon suggest women's magazines inspired localized stories for the original "WOMENEWS" prototype, during my group interview with Brown, Joyce, Franz, and Rudolph, they indicated that local stories were not at the heart of the new section. Instead, they all agreed, the content included mostly news about women around the world. This global perspective, according to

Franz, was strategically associated with economics and marketing at the *Tribune*. Editors constructed "Woman News" for syndication and sold it to other newspapers across the nation. One report estimates that about sixty newspapers signed on during its first year (Hansen 1992). Brown said from the start "Woman News" was supposed to be like a newspaper in and of itself. Franz concurred: "I think the idea was that it was supposed to be able to run in any newspaper in the world or in the country" (Franz 2002). Because of this marketing strategy, the original iteration of "Woman News" did not have a lot of Chicago-specific content. An early publication deadline typical of feature sections added to the difficulty of creating timely local stories. "Woman News" was printed the Sunday before it hit newsstands and production was the Thursday before that. This advanced deadline of about ten days before publication and stories planned a month in advance of that did not only create difficulties in covering timely local news but, editors said, it caused the section to be "stagnant."

Franz explained that by constructing "Woman News" for syndication, the section offered the *Tribune* significant marketing value. Typically about sixteen pages, the section had an editor, two-and-a-half assistant editors, and a columnist devoted to the section. Freelance writers and syndicated columnists provided additional content. The highly formatted section covered development of legislation for women and what various women had done for different causes, according to Franz and others. Family and parenting stories and a "survival guide" that included such tips as how to change a flat tire were also found in "Woman News." Joyce, who now edits a weekly health and family section, explained that before the family section started there were a lot of family and parenting stories in "Woman News." She said that was "because it was the only place for them" (Joyce 2002). As for the tone of the newly formed "Woman News," Brown, Joyce, Rudolph, and Franz all remembered it in a similar way. They described it as having a "harder edge," being "feminist," and with a "strident tone." Franz explained, "It was really kind of up there and in your face" (Franz 2002).

Two recent academic studies about the *Tribune*'s "Woman News" offer further insight. Hawley (1997) examined the creation and perceptions of "Woman News" during its first forty months. Through in-depth interviews with four key staff members and two focus groups with a total of eighteen female *Tribune* subscribers, she examined the ability of a woman's section to attract and keep women readers and also explored a women's sections inherent value to the mainstream press. Hawley (1997) said that founding editor Marjorie David believed "Woman News" was necessary for women because of their unequal status within the newspaper industry. David is quoted as saying "Any minority is going to be powerless unless it has a voice, and that's what we're doing is providing a voice. Or providing a physical sounding board, a place, a focus where we are covering stories that weren't getting done. . . . Women weren't at the table to bring them into the discussion. We started to push the door a little wider open" (Hawley 1997, 9). But even if the editors at the *Tribune* believed a women's section rectified a wrong,

Hawley also found that staff members and readers had mixed and often conflicting reactions to "Woman News." David, whose beliefs were unpopular in the news-room, explained, "Our biggest problem is our fellow journalists" (Hawley 1997, 10). Another of Hawley's interview subjects believed in the necessity of women's sections in the 1990s, but noted how others including David's successor, Marilyn Krause, and Barbara Brotman, a "Woman News" columnist, had both opposed the creation of the section. Hawley (1997) summarized that the problem with the sec-tion was that it "resurrected memories of coverage they had once worked hard to leave behind earlier in their journalistic careers" (Hawley 1997, 11). Krause and Brotman, who both made some positive points about "Woman News," believed organizing news by gender promoted stereotypical notions of women. David, who edited the section through September 1993, however, expressed wonder that in-cluding the name "woman" in the section title "caused considerable consternation among some journalists and readers" (Hawley 1997, 9).

During Hawley's focus groups she found participants expressed opposition to the use "woman" in the section title, complaining that it virtually guaranteed men would not read it (Hawley 1997). Ultimately, though, Hawley's focus groups revealed what other focus groups had: Women disagreed with the concept of a women's sections but ultimately enjoyed "Woman News." Hawley (1997) con-cluded her study by declaring that "women's sections play an important role in increasing the visibility of women in the mainstream newspaper, giving once-marginal readers a voice, and creating for women a sense of connection and iden-tification with others—a community not only of women but of people" (21). But Hawley notes unwanted consequences for naming a section for women, including "men won't be exposed to issues that are—or should be—the concern of both women and men," women journalists' work is ghettoized, and advertising in these sections stereotype women and "underscore women's weaknesses instead of their strengths" (Hawley 1997, 21–22).

A more recent investigation into the launch of the *Tribune*'s "Woman News" attempted to determine whether it was replicating traditional women's pages or offering something new and valuable (Lueck and Chang 2002). The author's analysis takes a cultural feminist approach, "which recognizes the importance of a separate women's space within male-defined culture for the nurturance of women's own culture and voice" (59). The authors used principles of women's media developed by the Women's Institute for Freedom of the Press, to decide whether "Woman News" could be deemed "women's media." These included, women speaking in their own voices, media that pay "attention to the representa-tion of women in mainstream media and analyzed the effects of exclusion and ste-reotypical portrayal of women," "a wider acceptance of different types of women beyond the narrow confines of the cultural ideal," and "an activist approach, or calls for feminist action" (59–60). After examining content in the section during the first year, Lueck and Chang (2002) found positive results for all four criteria. They concluded that "Woman News" introduced women's media into the media mainstream and "indicated the sorely inadequate nature of newspapers' ability to address women, women's needs and contemporary issues" (68). While the study offers valuable insight, editors in 2002 said the current "Woman News" was very different than what had been published during the first year, which is the content that Lueck and Chang studied.

"News for Today's Women" Debuts in Lexington

In December 1991, following the unveiling of the "WOMANEWS" prototype, a Knight-Ridder Women Readers Task Force presented the report "How Newspapers Can Gain Readership Among Women . . . And Why It's Important" (Kelly 1992, 12). Knight-Ridder, one of the nation's largest newspaper publishers at the time, conducted one-on-one interviews with 154 women in seven cities (Knight-Ridder 1991). The report offered newspapers information on women's reading desires and shopping habits and suggestions for making newspapers more appealing to women. Rather than present one way for all newspapers to increase the appeal of their paper to women, the report suggested newspapers' conduct local reader interviews. The report also recommended each newspaper examines its own pages and newsroom for female representation. Filled with content recommendations based on what women expressed caring about, the report urged newspapers to fix the entire paper by adding the missing content women desired. The report, however, also indicated that adding a section for women was a progressive solution. *Lexington Herald-Leader* general manager and chair of the ASNE Future of Newspapers Committee, Scott McGhee, believed contemporary women's section were a necessary step in regaining female readers.[3] While once opposed to women's pages, in the report McGhee explained her belief that because of the realities in the newspaper industry and the differences between men and women, the special sections are necessary. She wrote:

> if I have learned anything over the years, it is to be comfortable with one fact of life: Women and men are different. We are not different, of course, in intelligence or ability or energy or most of our news and information interests. (I include this blindingly obvious statement only because if I don't, some dunce of one gender or another will misunderstand.) We do continue to lead somewhat different lives, whether or not it's right or fair. Women still have the lioness's share of responsibility for childcare and home care and care of aging parents. Women still face different treatment and obstacles in the workplace. Women have gender-specific health concerns. (Knight-Ridder 1991, 7)

With this in mind, McGhee directed staff at the *Herald-Leader*, a Knight-Ridder paper, to develop a section for "at-risk female readers" (Kelly 1992). After conducting interviews and focus groups, the *Herald-Leader* staff defined their at-risk female readers as under thirty years old and likely to in the last three years have done at least one of the following: changed marital status, become a mother, changed the number of workers in her household, changed employment status or moved, and she "feels harried and unable to control events" (Kelly 1992, 13).

On Sunday, April 2, 1992 the *Herald-Leader* published its first issue of "You," a weekly inserted tabloid section subtitled "News for Today's Woman." The *Herald-Leader* put not only energy into its new section, but also money. In an article then editor and vice president Tim Kelly explained how the new section received a budget of $125,000 for newsprint, staff, recruiting, training, the purchase of syndicated material, and even the production of a TV advertisement for "You" (Kelly 1992). In a May/June 1992 issue of the *ASNE Bulletin* Kelly said readers had responded positively to the new section with letters and calls running about ten to one in favor of it. Along with targeting women with particular content, the reporters of "You" were expected to write differently as well, to accommodate women who said they were pressed for time. Kelly (1992) described the way of writing as "not prose and not how reporters are traditionally trained to write. It's all very much to the point, straightforward and as clear and concise as possible" (14). Paula Anderson, who in 2002 worked in human resources for the *Herald-Leader*, helped conduct research for "You" and served as features editor for the paper from 1988 through 1995. Anderson said she looked at women's magazines to guide the development of "You." At the start, Anderson recalled, the section focused on health and family, shopping, and consumer concerns. "You" also included a standing feature titled "One Woman's Story," which was an abbreviated profile of a local woman.

Tim Kelly, who as editor oversaw the development of "You," was the publisher at the *Herald-Leader* in 2002. He remembers the concern executives had over the male and female readership statistics. In the early 1990s, he said, 57 percent of males surveyed in the newspaper's readership area had read the paper the previous day while only 43 percent of females had. But, he said, in keeping with the overall recommendation of the Knight-Ridder report, the *Herald-Leader* editors instituted a number of changes to attract more women readers. One problem Kelly worked to rectify was the paper's "very decidedly male management cast" (Kelly 2002). At the time, he said, only one woman served on the management team and there were only three or four female department heads. And, he explained, two of these women were occupying traditional female roles—one as the head librarian and another as features editor. Kelly believed this lack of women in decision-making positions contributed to the lower rate of women readers because story selection and the tone of content were filtered through male sensibilities. Kelly and other executives made an effort to change these problems while adding the women's section. Mike Johnson, the newspaper's deputy managing editor in 2002 and the assistant managing editor when production of "You" began, explained,

There was kind of this debate as, OK, if you want to attract female readers, how do you do it? Do you do it in a section specifically targeting at risk female readers or do you do it by, you know, do it throughout the newspaper? And, I think kind of the thinking, at least here, turned out to be, well, you do it both ways. You may have a section targeted at female readers, but you also want to make sure that you are thinking about female readers, using female sources, that type of thing, throughout your newspaper and throughout your coverage. (Johnson 2002)

Anderson concurred, explaining that, "There was an exercise or an effort to really look at the mix on the front page to try to get more female faces on the paper, to try to be very conscious of those things" (Anderson 2002).

Anderson remembered how a section targeting women stimulated discomfort among staff in the newsroom. Kelly acknowledged the concern some staff had too but still justified the decision. He explained:

I've lived through all of the concern that, well you're just, all you're doing is just ghettoizing, you know, women's news, and, you know, you're taking women back to the days when women's news was only society news and women only write soft features and all that stuff. And you know we were doing a whole lot of other things in the newsroom too, to diversify the content of the paper. So this was just part of it. It was just probably the most noticeable and visible part. (Kelly 2002)

Introducing "Savvy" to Women and Women to Advertisers

Four years after the *Herald-Leader* introduced its weekly women's pages *The Capital Times* in Madison, Wisconsin, re-evaluated its features section. The paper decided on the popular thematic approach in its features pages and like the *Tribune* and *Herald-Leader* focused sections around topics during different days of the week, including a day devoted to women. In each of the daily sections standing features—comics, advice columns, the TV guide, and entertainment reviews—were published. The women's section, called "Savvy" with the subtitle "News for Today's Women," hit the newsstands each Thursday. From the start, along with the standing copy mentioned above, the section offered one or two front-page features, an inside feature dedicated to a local woman ("Savvy Snapshot"), another regular feature dubbed "Savvy Shopper," a few local and national columns written by women, and a calendar of events relevant to women. "Savvy Shopper" covered a broad range of topics, including advice on how to save money, consumer issues, and fashion news. Family and parenting stories and advice columns filled pages of the newly developed "Savvy" along with stories detailing women in nontraditional roles.

The Capital Times introduced "Savvy" on September 7, 1995, but only after serious debate and the same kind of mixed opinions and resistance that staff expressed at the *Chicago Tribune* and *Lexington Herald-Leader*, according to both newsroom mythology and several editors and reporters who were present at the time. The features editor in 2001, Mary Bergin, said women in the newsroom did not exactly support the idea because they worried it would stereotype women and marginalize content. A copy editor in 2001 Judy Ettenhofer, who worked as assistant city editor when "Savvy" first appeared, recalled the discomfort women in the newsroom felt with a women's section. As a woman in the newsroom, Ettenhofer said, she was afraid the section would be filled with "fluffy" content and portray women as obsessed with their looks and interested in little else.

According to an article published in the first edition of "Savvy," focus groups helped the paper to understand what local women wanted in their daily newspaper. The article began with an explanation of the purpose behind "Savvy," explaining that it was "part of our effort to appeal to more women readers" (Maeglin 1995). But at *The Capital Times*, unlike the *Lexington Herald-Leader*, few people talked about offering women missing content. A sentence in the introductory article explicitly described the motivation behind the paper's effort: "Women are the primary consumers in most households these days. So newspapers, like any other business, have to try harder to reach them" (Maeglin 1995). Clayton Frink, who in 2001 had been the paper's publisher for the last seven years, acknowledged that economics drove the paper to reintroduce a women's section. But Frink also talked in depth about how newspapers had lost women readers by ignoring them. He explained that during the course of his career "I saw a lot of research and went to a lot of meetings, and I guess it struck a chord with me that newspapers are generally edited—and this has not been absolutely true for a long time, but still, even as the '60s and '70s changed a lot of attitudes in America, newspapers still look a lot like they had before the '60s, which were edited for, [and] by white males" (Frink 2001). Explaining that the research he saw "struck a chord," Frink wanted to move away from the all "white male" content and suggested the women's section. Still throughout his discussion about providing women readers with relevant content, Frink often went back to the market value of such a move. Finally, he explained, "I hope it wasn't crass, but I made a remark earlier about what's right and what's marketable. My job is to help find what's marketable. If it happens to be right, that's cool" (Frink 2001). In other words, Frink made it clear that the bottom line for introducing "Savvy" was financial.

Field Interviews

To better understand contemporary newsroom perspectives about women's sections, I interviewed thirty-five publishers, editors, reporters, a copy editor, and various other people working in five newsrooms. The interviews took place at three newspapers producing new women's pages—*Chicago Tribune, Lexington Herald-Leader*, and *Capital Times*—and two other newspapers—*Wisconsin State Journal* and *Milwaukee Journal Sentinel*—where feature sections have remained under non-sex–specific headings.[4] When possible, the interviews were conducted one-on-one outside of the immediate newsroom environment, often over meals or coffee.[5] In one instance during my research, an informal group interview at the *Chicago Tribune* took the place of individual interviews. In this case, the group setting offered the only opportunity to gain access to key people within the newsroom. Informal discussions and varying amounts of observation—dependent on the amount of access given—also took place in the newsrooms. During my observations I focused on how decisions about the women's pages and the paper's front page were made, from story assignments and development to design.

I identified major or large metropolitan daily U.S. newspapers that published weekly women's pages or sections—defined as newspaper pages that explicitly target women readers.[6] Newspapers make this explicit claim by either naming the section for women (as in the *Chicago Tribune*'s "Woman News" section) or using a subtitle for the section that claims to offer content to women (as in the *Lexington Herald-Leader*'s "You—News for Today's Women"). From the list of newspapers found in this initial exploration, I chose three newspapers with weekly women's sections—*Chicago Tribune*, *Lexington Herald-Leader*, and *Capital Times*.

I chose the *Chicago Tribune* because of its circulation size (the sixth largest in the country), status in the newspaper industry, and because it was one of the first U.S. newspapers to reintroduce women's pages to readers. At the time of my interviews, in 2001 and 2002, the *Chicago Tribune* had a daily paid circulation of about 658,000 and a Sunday paid circulation of 1,046,000. It delivers to a more diverse readership than the other papers in the study simply because of Chicago's population size and diversity. But because of the large suburban sprawl around Chicago, the paper does not target only a highly urban readership. The circulation size of the *Tribune* translates into large papers and the ability to publish a depth of content equal to only a handful of newspapers in the county.[7] The Kentucky paper was also chosen for study because it too introduced a contemporary women's section early (in 1992). The *Lexington Herald-Leader* has a daily paid circulation of about 114,000 and a Sunday paid circulation of about 155,000. After contacting the *Lexington Herald-Leader*, I learned that the paper's publisher was in the process of eliminating the women's section after ten years of publication, making it an especially interesting case. *The Capital Times* became part of the study because its inclusion offered the opportunity to study a smaller newspaper. The afternoon-published *Capital Times* offers "Savvy—News for Today's Women." *The Capital Times* is an afternoon daily with a weekday paid circulation of about 20,000 and a Saturday paid circulation of about 23,000.

To offer industry context and better understand how news workers conceptualize and frame contemporary women's pages in relation to more common feature sections, I chose to conduct interviews at two newspapers without women's pages. I chose the *Wisconsin State Journal* in Madison, Wisconsin.[8] The *Wisconsin State Journal*, the state's second largest daily newspaper, has a daily paid circulation of about 90,000 a Sunday paid circulation of about 160,000. I also conducted interviews at the *Milwaukee Journal Sentinel*. Created in 1995 when two long-published Milwaukee papers merged, the *Milwaukee Journal Sentinel* is the largest and most-read paper in Wisconsin with a daily paid circulation size of 250,000 and a Sunday circulation size of 450,000. While the newspaper does not specifically publish women's pages, during my visits to the newsroom I found that the possibility was being discussed. This fact made this newspaper an excellent addition to the book.

The interviews took place between September 2001 and February 2002.[9] In the features department at *The Capital Times* I interviewed the publisher, editor, features editors, and reporters. Three editors and four reporters make up the features department, though a number of other local and national writers contribute columns to these pages. One of these editors is the "Savvy" editor. At the *Chicago Tribune* I interviewed the "Woman News" editor and a regular columnist for the section and observed a "Woman News" staff meeting. I also interviewed two associate managing editors of features and three additional high-level features department editors—including one who had been a "Woman News" editor. At the *Lexington Herald-Leader* the editor assigned someone to coordinate my visit. As it turned out the editor had spent quite a deal of time thinking about women readers and women's pages and welcomed my research in the area. The willingness on the part of the *Herald-Leader* to participate in my work and to allow me to interview people from various aspects of the paper meant I was able to compile especially rich information in a short time. The features staff at the *Herald-Leader* consists of an editor, two assistants, and several reporters and writers. At the *Herald-Leader* I met with the features editor, two assistant features editors, assistant managing editor, the publisher (who had been editor during the launch of the paper's women section "You"), and a features reporter. I also interviewed a former features editor who currently heads human resources (and worked on the original "You"), the marketing research manager, and the advertising supervisor.[10]

This chapter details why the newspaper industry again considered producing explicitly named women's pages after about twenty years without them. Newspapers had lost women readers and were attempting to get them back, because a female readership is essential to advertising revenue. To solve its problem, industry leaders turned to the same solution their predecessors had a century earlier. With that decision, contemporary women's pages were born. Details from three newsrooms where this occurred offer a deeper understanding of why and how these contemporary women's sections came about. The next three chapters detail my discoveries. Chapter five details the many ways in which journalists creating women's pages define the content, and also shows what some journalists without women's pages think of "women's news."

Notes

1. The readership gap, however, varies widely by the circulation size of the paper (Miller 1998). She explains, "While large metros commonly face male-female readership differences of 10-to-15 percentage points, double-digit gaps rarely occur at under-twenty five thousand-circulation dailies, which make up some 70 percent of the 1,520 U.S. daily newspapers. However, the top twenty metros account for roughly one-quarter of total U.S. daily newspaper circulation, and that big-city circulation skews overall readership statistics" (Miller 1998, 44). Miller accounts for this aspect of the readership gap by explaining that "Smaller papers base their livelihoods on community news and providing news and information that helps residents with community problems" (44). Surveys have shown that this is the type of news women want in a newspaper.

2. The *Chicago Tribune*'s weekly section was titled "Womanews" though in his article, Kelly talks about "WOMENEWS," which was the title of the prototype. In additional articles, the *Tribune*'s section is referred to as "WomaNews" and "WomanNews." Eventually the *Tribune* editors changed the name to "Woman News" with a space between the two words. Throughout the study, I use this one means of referring to the section in order to avoid confusion.

3. Scott McGehee is a woman. I make this note because I believe it is of interest to know the gender of those who were developing and promoting sections targeting women and this information may not be immediately known because "Scott" is often a man's name. The information is relevant as some argue the development of contemporary women's pages is a way for male editors to satisfy women readers without integrating women into all areas of a newspaper.

4. The interviews were conducted using a short list of open-ended questions, which allowed for a conversation partially directed by the interviewee. Feminist methodologies informed my research design. Feminist scholars argue for circumventing the traditional interviewing process based on "a masculine paradigm, embedded in a masculine culture and stressing masculine traits while at the same time excluding traits such as sensitivity, emotionality, and others that are culturally viewed as feminine traits" (Fontana and Frey 2000, 658). The open-ended nature of the questions and ability for the interviewer to let the "conversation" direct further questions, allowed me to discover points of interest that may not have materialized in an otherwise highly structured interview setting (Fontana and Frey 2000, 652). This was particularly useful considering that much of this research is focused on how newspaper workers do their work.

5. Oakley (1981) criticizes the interview process for not considering gendered differences. She points out that the interview as a form of information gathering in social science research has been approached from a nongender perspective that treats both the

interviewers and the respondents as faceless and genderless entities. This is important as Denzin (1989) notes, because "gender filters knowledge" (116). Fontana and Frey (2000) elaborate, "the sex of the interviewer and that of the respondent do make a difference, as the interview takes place within the cultural boundaries of a paternalistic social system in which masculine identities are differentiated from feminine ones" (658). Other identities—including a person's race or ethnicity, class, age and level of education—also contribute to the interaction and filtering of knowledge (Behar 1996; Collins 1990). Critics of traditional methods call for researchers to be aware of how the identity of an interviewer shapes the interviewing process and knowledge gained. I am aware that my presence as a white, highly educated, middle-class mother in her early 30s, had an impact on the information I gathered, and that researchers of other identities would experience differently what I experienced during my data collection. Just how my identity shaped the research would only be speculation but should be understood in the context of the environment where I conducted my research. I believe gender, race/ethnicity, and age—those identities typically understood through visual cues—had the most impact on my research. Gender issues, as well as talk about feminism and the women's movement, almost always came up in interviews and typically without direct questions in these areas. I presume that had a man been asking the same questions, the answers may have been less focused on women and gender. My role of parent, and particularly working mother, seemed to inspire more conversation in this area. When I was asked if I had children, I answered honestly. This tended to inspire conversation related to parenting, family, and the particular difficulties of working parents—especially mothers and those that are single. These, of course, are instances when I presume my identity mattered, but it's likely there are plenty of other instances I am unaware of.

6. I chose to do a collective case study, believing that the cases together lead to a better understanding and perhaps theorizing of the newspaper industry in general (Stake 1994, 237).

7. The *Tribune* first began publishing a contemporary women's section in 1989 (called "Tempo Woman") and in 1991 launched a revised version titled "Woman News"; however as of 2005 it had been abolished.

8. The *State Journal* actually publishes through a joint operating agreement with *The Capital Times*. The two newspapers, a morning and afternoon paper, share advertising and marketing but have separate news staffs and editorial content. The morning daily *State Journal* has not instituted women's pages while the afternoon published *Capital Times* offers "Savvy—News for Today's Women" on a weekly basis. *The Capital Times* promotes itself as the more liberal of the two Madison newspapers. In fact, across the masthead, the paper claims to be "Dane County's Progressive Newspaper."

9. Audio recordings of the interviews were made with the permission of those interviewed. The interviewees were also asked to sign a consent form that explained their ability to ask for anonymity at any time during the interview or the comments would be attached to their identity. None of the subjects asked for anonymity. The newspapers were not offered anonymity as I felt the study would be more valuable with the names of the newspapers intact.

10. Along with attending a morning news meeting, I was trained on and allowed to search the paper's electronic morgue.

Chapter 5
Conceptualizing and Constructing Contemporary Women

This chapter explores more deeply how contemporary news workers conceptualize and construct the newest iteration of women's pages. When industry leaders became concerned with a decrease in female readership during the late 1980s and into the 1990s, many argued that a contemporary section specifically targeting women would bring women readers back to newspapers. The solution was based on the notion that women had turned away from daily newspapers because newspapers did not offer relevant content to women and that women did not see themselves in the newspapers. With this in mind, a number of newspapers developed sections specifically for women. But this solution presented contemporary publishers, editors, and reporters with a dilemma: how to define women's content. This chapter illustrates the various ways in which editors and reporters constructing these modern day women's pages have reconciled this predicament. It also offers perspectives from news workers who work on traditional style or feature sections. The various viewpoints show just how difficult it is to define news content by sex or gender and underscore the blurred boundaries between the various sections of newspapers. Finally the chapter examines more deeply the complexities inherent in defining news by sex, including the dangers of stereotyping women and presenting them in narrow terms. What is clear through the words of these publishers, editors, and reporters is that many have given a great deal of thought to the topic of "women's news" and that a multitude of perspectives about the topic exist.

Defining "Women's News"

When asked what constitutes "women's news," editors and reporters gave various answers but their answers fell into four broad categories. "Women's news" was defined by topic, in opposition to past women's sections, by audience, and through writing style. Often the same person would define the content for women using more than one of these strategies. What became clear in most of the discussions and according to most of the definitions was that women's news could be just about anything. There were, however, a set of topics that continually surfaced in my conversations. These were not surprising either and mimic the topics seen in original women's pages, those that fall within the private sphere and engage the typical idea about what is important to women. Among those story topics most often heard: health, relationships, fashion, advice columns, and parenting and family. Paula Anderson, a features editor at the *Lexington Herald-Leader* during the launch of "You," explained that when "You" came out "We much more focused on health and family and shopping, lots of consumer kinds of things" (Anderson 2002).

But many of those I talked to said women's news included topics related to the public domain that contemporary women occupy. This is not surprising considering working mothers at one point became the primary target audience for all three of the women's sections. A typical example of this occurred in my conversation with Phil Haslanger, the managing editor at *The Capital Times* where "Savvy" had been published for several years. When asked to define "women's news" in general, without hesitation Haslanger offered these examples: pay equity, harassment in the workplace, violence against women, breaking barriers, dealing with the stresses of juggling home, family and elder care, and women's health issues like breast cancer. This idea of dealing with the difficulties of working outside the home while maintaining family and domestic responsibilities came up often. Debra Carr-Elsing, lead writer for "Savvy," explained that the section was filled with "a lot of issues relating to working women today as well as children's pieces" (Carr-Elsing 2001).

The *Tribune*'s Brotman offered examples in her attempt to define women's news. Those included an in-depth article about self-breast exams and stories about abortion. Pointing to an example in a recent "Woman News" edition, she explained, "The story about abortion, it's a story of greater interest to women. Women are the ones who might be in a situation where they'd be questioning whether or not to get an abortion. So it is just that women will pay more attention to that" (Brotman 2002). Jim Higgins, an assistant features editor, at the *Milwaukee Journal Sentinel*, where explicitly named women's pages do not exist, was acutely aware of the complicated nature of naming news content by gender. When I asked him if there was such a thing as women's news, and if so to define it, he said: "Anything I say would be a hopeless generalization that you'll smear me with later. I'll sadly start in the traditional place. The personal [and] how it affects daily life . . . family, relationships . . . and in the broad sense they are a lot of the same kinds of concerns that you would find in women's stuff of 30 years ago" (Higgins 2002).

Often those interviewed defined content for these contemporary women's section in opposition to "traditional" women's sections, explaining that these newly developed women's section do not offer the same content a reader would find in women's pages prior to the 1970s. Phil Haslanger, *The Capital Times* managing editor in 2001, explained the plan at his paper was to focus on women "but not in the traditional women's sense—recipes and fashions—but talking about women's issues in the workplace and with families and such. It was more savvy, I guess, to reflect contemporary women as opposed to women of the past" (Haslanger 2001). When asked specifically to define "Savvy" content, he again relied on a relational explanation while citing topics: "It's aimed at issues in women's lives more than handy tips for living at home. That it tries to focus on issues women face in society, in the workplace, in their families, but less on a, less as a 'Good Housekeeping' sort of focus" (Haslanger 2001). This discussion of "Savvy" as constructed in opposition to traditional women's pages, came up in numerous conversations with those working in the newsroom. Carr-Elsing (2001), also at *The Capital Times*, explained, "The whole definition has changed. To me the women, when we're thinking of the old-time, stereotypical women's section was actually a society page, . . . it was kind of a women's slash society news that was real fluff." Talking about "You" at the *Lexington Herald-Leader*, Tim Kelly (2002) explained (in the past tense because the women's pages were being eliminated), "Traditional women's sections had nothing but cooking and sewing and home life and all that stuff. I mean, we were addressing work issues, relationship issues, how, you know, juggling your time issues. There was no question it was an updated version of the, a modern version of the women's section to address the changes in women's lives since the '50s and '60s" (Kelly 2002).

When I asked Wendy Navratil, the *Chicago Tribune*'s "Woman News" editor in 2002, to define women's news, she explained: "I don't think that there is a topic and I don't even necessarily think it's the way it's written. I think the only thing that, or your guiding principal, is that you know that women are your readers" (Navratil 2002). This definition seems to allow for and justify placing any news content in a women's section. In fact, Navratil acknowledges this fact, explaining "women are your readers and you can speak to them about things that interest them, which now is so all over the map" (Navratil 2002). Navratil's answer also highlights how complicated the task is. Through my conversation with Navratil it became obvious that she wanted the section she edited to be taken seriously, not to be seen in the way traditional women's pages had been. She did not want to limit her content through topical definitions, nor did she want to narrowly define women's interests. It also reflected a view consistent with those who actually answered my question by explaining that they did not believe something called "women's news" could be defined. When asked, "Do you think there is such a thing as women's news?" Nicole Rogers, the assistant features editor at the *Wisconsin State Journal* where explicit women's pages are not published, explained: "People think so. I think there's such a thing as stories that will have specific readers and, you know, they can be drawn on gender lines, they can be drawn on class lines, they can be drawn on racial lines. They're going to attract specific readers and, you know, it's hard to say, because I would think some stories are more interesting to women, but then again, some stories are more interesting to men" (Rogers 2002).

Some of those I asked to define "women's news" explained that it was not the topic or whom a writer thinks of when they are constructing a story but rather the way in which the story is written. This explanation emphasizes a reality in news writing. That is to say, that for many topics in the newspaper, it is the writing style that determines placement not the particular topic. This explanation highlights the hard/soft split traditionally seen in news content. In talking with four of the main features editors at the *Chicago Tribune* about how they define women's news, one recalled a story about Koky Dishon, who had worked for the *Tribune* for years. She said:

> She came in and had done something like a Tempo [feature section] story and she had started, she was like the features editor of the paper and they complained that "you took that story and that should have been in news." She said she went back to her office and she rewrote that story for sports, for business, for main news, for features and she said it's strictly in the angle that you take. And I guess, I've always thought that and she really vocalized it. I think that with "Woman News" there's probably not a story that you could not, a sports story, a business story, it just depends on the approach that you take. I don't look at areas of coverage for "Woman News," I think of approach. (Joyce 2002)

In fact, this idea of the arbitrary boundaries drawn between different sections in a newspaper came up often. This was particularly true when I presented my interview participants with story examples and asked them to tell me which section of the newspaper the story belonged. My story scenarios included an abortion clinic bombing, and stories about women in sports and politics. Rather than simply name a section, typically the person I was talking to would explain the various focuses the story could take and ways it might fit into various sections.

Content Boundaries and Contradictions

The various ways publishers, editors, and reporters define women's news stresses the complicated nature of the task. Many of those I interviewed acknowledged this while there were others who contradicted themselves throughout our conversation, seemly without even realizing it. The contradictions were another indication of the inherent complexities associated with creating newspaper content for a sex specific audience. One of the most obvious contradictions occurred when editors and reporters named traditionally gendered topics to define "women's news" but at the same time maintained that these contemporary sections were constructed in opposition to the traditional ones. A couple of explanations help in understanding how this perspective exists within the newsroom. For one, those who were describing these traditional sections as filled with only traditional "soft" news stories and society news, likely did not actually read them. Either the people I talked with were women who were not reading newspapers before the creation of modern day feature sections (pre–1969) or they were older men in upper editorial positions within the newsroom who twenty or more years earlier were not reading the women's sections because they were women's sections. The common belief is that these women's sections only carried food, fashion, furnishings, and family content, but few realized important and serious stories were also published in these spaces. With that in mind, it seems these contemporary topics and sections are more similar than some realize. Probably the biggest difference in terms of content, however, is the focus on the working mother versus the stay-at-home mother.

Another reoccurring theme that offered a contradictory view of these contemporary women's pages was that while these sections were targeting women, they were also for men. So while the editors and reporters believed there were topics or ways of writing that might appeal more to women than men, they felt that this was not a rule but only a guide used to fill the pages. Clayton Frink, the publisher at *The Capital Times*, made this point in what seemed mostly to be a justification for having a women's section and acknowledgment of the risks involved. He said:

> I think the reason we haven't done more, and the reason things are done the way they are as opposed to some other way, is because there's a bit of political correctness. There's a risk of talking down to a segment of the population when you say this is especially for you. I think that would be wrong. I think it's also wrong to suggest—and I don't think I'd alter my words at all if you were a male researcher—I think it would be wrong to say, we're going to edit this just for women. The point is to be conscious of some of the ways things have been done that may be exclusionary. [You need to be] conscious of a different perspective on things and try to include that as well, so that you cover everything. You don't want to produce something that men aren't interested in as well, that's not very good marketing to drive one segment away in order to bring in another. (Frink 2001)

Carr-Elsing believed that while she was writing for women, the "Savvy" section had a large male readership. She explained that often when she tells interview subjects that the story will be published in "Savvy, the women's section," people are surprised. She said that they "say 'women's section, well don't tell my husband that because that's his favorite section of the paper, he always reads Savvy.' And they don't believe it's a women's section. People don't even notice the phrase on the masthead of that section that says 'News for today's women,'" (Carr-Elsing 2001). Carr-Elsing said she believed men read the section regularly because the issues were of interest to them as well. Among those topics, she named women in business, childcare, home organization, and communication skills.

In my conversation with Chris Juzwik, the feature's section editor at the *Wisconsin State Journal*, he mentioned regularly reading the *Chicago Tribune*'s "Woman News" section. I asked him specifically why a man would read a section labeled for women and he explained "I guess I like to find out what women might be interested in or what kinds of stories are being targeted for women on the news. I'm very curious about that" (Juzwik 2002). Part of his interest, then, was as an editor and newsroom worker. But he continued, saying he would be interested in knowing "what sorts of topics make women tick."

Stereotyping Women?

Reporters and editors at each of the papers talked about news and information that might help women live their lives more easily as being an important part of their section's content. From this perspective most of the definitions of women's news—whether described using topics, an oppositional description, audience, or writing style—rested on an understanding that women are different from men. The belief in men and women's essential difference was most often based in an understanding of cultural differences. For example that women are most often the primary caregivers, shoppers, and cooks in a household.

There were times, however, when the differences were described as biological. Amy Mertz, "Savvy's" editor, took an essentialist approach when defining "women's news" and women and men's differences. But even while she pointed to "biological" distinctions and "instinct," some of the issues of interest that she brought up were rooted in cultural realities. For example she talked about violence against women. She said:

> Women and men have different biological and different kinds of instincts. Women seem to be a little more nurturing and it's hard to not stereotype in that way. Because of that I think they're interested in hearing different things. They do want to hear about safety issues, protecting themselves; they want to hear about violence against women; they want to know what's being done to combat violence against women. They want to hear about health issues, about activism, and there's just so much to learn. I also think they want to see positive examples of women in the community who are doing good things, and that's most of it. (Mertz 2001)

My conversation with Mertz was not the only time I heard stereotypical or essentialized notions of women. Often it was unclear whether the essentialist image of women came out of a belief in biological differences or in the distinct cultural experiences of women. What was clear, however, was that those who espoused these gender differences believed them to be unproblematic and often pointed to readership studies as providing evidence for women's unique reading interests. With this in mind, and considering that women's sections exist as the only thematic features sections that actually targets an audience with a description of that audience, editors and reporters were asked to comment on whether or not they felt a concern for stereotyping women through the construction of "women's news." Many of the respondents answered the question with little reflection and quickly changed the subject. The *Lexington Herald-Leader*'s deputy managing editor at the time and the assistant managing editor during the launch of "You," Mike Johnson, offered a typical response. He explained:

> I don't recall that we did [worry about reinforcing gender stereotypes]. I mean, you know, our real focus was just to always think of, you know, stories that might attract women readers and, at that time, all of our features editors were female. And, so, you know, our main goal was just to try and think of, you know, things that one would attract them to the newspaper, but, two, also provide them with the kind of information they might need or want that would help make their life easier for them or at least less hectic in some ways. (Johnson 2002)

Paula Anderson, the features editor at the *Herald-Leader* when "You" began, did not reflect much on the question either and also turned the conversation toward the goals at the time. When asked, "Did you ever worry about reinforcing gender stereotypes?" she said, "Yeah, I mean I grew up thinking you should not do women's sections, and so when all this came out, I thought geez, what are we gonna do this for?' What I think I tried to do with it was to take it and experiment with it and learn from it. What we'd hoped, you know, is that we would see this huge jump in female readership" (Anderson 2002).

Geoff Brown, associate managing editor of features at the *Tribune* in 2002, did not answer the question directly but instead justified the section, explaining, "My feeling is that it goes back to what someone said earlier, that there wasn't enough of this stuff in other sections" (Brown 2002). Other editors at the *Tribune* explained that the section's diversity prevented it from being stereotypical, explaining that stories were about all types of women. The two most contemplative answers regarding stereotyping women through women's pages came from the *Tribune*'s thirty-two-year-old "Woman News" editor, Wendy Navratil, and twenty-five-year-old Amy Mertz, *The Capital Times*' "Savvy" editor. When asked if they worried about promoting stereotypes, both noted the importance of balancing their section's content in order to avoid stereotypes. Navratil said:

> We're always aware of trying to make sure that we don't, but I think we're moving past the knee-jerk reaction that to portray a woman as a mother is somehow to bring her down. I think that there is a big step forward in that you can cover women in all different capacities and you don't have to be afraid of the message that one story will send as long as all your stories are balancing out. We're doing a lot more about women who stay at home or women who are very religious. We've done stories about Christian denominations where women do believe in submitting to men and so we like to think we cover enough and are broad enough and keep all women in mind that no one story had to do everything or have this progressive message that if we're covering real people out there, it's worth doing. (Navratil 2002)

When asked if she worried about reinforcing gender stereotypes, Mertz responded, "Yes, definitely." But remember, Mertz also had talked about women's differences using the terms "biological" and "instinct." Mertz's discussion of stereotyping women hinted at the personal struggles she faces in constructing a section for women. After acknowledging she worries about gender stereotypes, Mertz offers one. She explained, "If there's a fashion story or something like that, you know, women like to shop and they're often the primary buyers in their house, but the least that we can do is try to put an interesting edge on it by maybe doing environmentally friendly places to shop, or something like that" (Mertz 2001). Mertz went on to explain how she rebelled against stereotyping women when she took over "Savvy." At the time she took responsibility for the section, a syndicated cartoon titled "Cathy" (authored by a woman) ran on the cover. She described the cartoon this way: "That was a constant stereotype. Every cartoon was aren't you fat, the mother was always saying 'When are you going to get married?' It was always about shopping, too much chocolate" (Mertz 2001). Mertz went to her editor in chief requesting to pull it but it was not until after he asked some of his women friends that he gave her permission. She explained: "He said, 'I just want to see what the general consensus is.' He came back and said, 'Nobody likes 'Cathy'" (Mertz 2002). Mertz also noted how difficult it is in her job to escape stereotyping women because of the realities of newsroom norms and routines, and particularly deadline pressures. Mertz explained "There are days when I go back and look at a section . . . when you look at the three [stories] together, you think, 'Oh, this could be perceived to be negative or old fashioned or whatever.' It happens by accident. I try to make a good effort of balance" (Mertz 2001). While Mertz certainly showed a concern about stereotypes—even if one complicated by contradictions—lead "Savvy" writer Debra Carr-Elsing said she does not worry about promoting gender stereotypes. When asked she echoed Navratil's point, saying, "No, because I think we're so diverse" (Carr-Elsing 2001). Later in our conversation, however, Carr-Elsing argued for the need for women's pages. In doing so, she presented an interesting stereotype about contemporary women, one that reinforces the feminist backlash premise and highlights the "fallacy" that women can have it all. She explained that "as women's roles in society changed they developed a second need for a women's section and it was tailored to appeal to the working woman of today and it's working women who are having troubles with infertility because they are not having children until their forties," (Carr-Elsing 2001).

Only *The Capital Times*' publisher, Clayton Frink, explaining that "Savvy" has certainly expanded its content beyond the traditional "society" sections, acknowledged the stereotypical nature of a women's section. Frink, however, makes no apology for the "fluff" found within "Savvy's" pages. He said it is not "quite as fluffy [as traditional women's pages], although there's obviously still room for fluff. Martha Stewart wouldn't be rich beyond all our wildest dreams if there wasn't a market for this kind of stuff, right?" (Frink 2001). On the other hand,

Paula Anderson at the *Lexington Herald-Leader* said the staff there consciously did not want the sections to be "silly and frivolous." To accomplish this, she said they tried to do a mix of stories "but we also knew that everybody loved that silly shopping column. I mean, it was who had the latest shipments in and, you know, there were specials on things and people just ate that up. I mean they just loved that" (Anderson 2002).

Defining, Discussing, and Dismissing Diversity

Editors and reporters at each of the newspapers were asked to talk about diversity in relation to their definition of women's news and their newspapers' women's sections. Respondents most often talked about age ranges of women, ranges of women's topics that they cover in their section, and parental status. Less frequently race or ethnicity, religion, and political perspective were brought up, though Phil Haslanger, managing editor at *The Capital Times*, immediately responded by saying, "Sometimes we focus on women from ethnic and racial minorities and the additional issues they may face." At no time did anyone mention sexual orientation reinforcing an understanding that these sections are constructed for a heterosexual woman. Mertz, editor of "Savvy," talked about age and parental status and only when prompted addressed other identity differences beyond these limited terms. She began by explaining that the lack of ethnic diversity in "Savvy" is "a reflection of life in Madison" (Mertz 2001). In reality, however, her vision reflected newspaper readers more than the population of Madison. The contradictory ideas and complexities surrounding diversity were clearly evident in her explanation and point to the difficulties newsroom staff sometimes confront in dealing with this issue. She said:

> I try not to overkill the whole diversity thing in "Savvy" or anywhere in the paper because I feel you want to be representative of the population and you don't want to be condescending to the population. If I were American Indian, I might be offended that people were trying so hard to win me over. I don't have anything to prove, and I don't think any of us do. When a story's there, it's there, and there's no need to force it. I do wish that there was more diversity because I think that we miss out on a lot of story ideas that way. We do have a communities reporter who is actually titled "ethnic" or "diversity" reporter—something like that—but we have someone who just focuses on neighborhoods and ethnic communities. She's been here a while and she has good connections, things like that help. We definitely don't make up for it, but that's as good as we can get right now. (Mertz 2001)

While Mertz begins her answer by defending the paper's lack of diversity as a reflection of the community, she finishes with an acknowledgment that the paper could do better. Especially interesting, however, is how Mertz admits she "might be offended" if a newspaper were trying so hard to win over a specific group of people yet she does not see the paper's focus on "women" in these same offensive terms. That she can more easily accept a women's section than a section for an ethnic group may stem from the fact that her job is to edit a women's section. She must reconcile any problems she might have with a women's section in order to adequately perform her job.

Barbara Brotman, a columnist for "Woman News" at the *Tribune*, talked about parenting, working mothers, and age when I asked her about diversity in the special section. I then specifically asked about ethnic diversity. She responded by acknowledging "I think it's mostly white and heavily suburban" but said it was an issue the editors were aware of and struggling to change (Brotman 2002). On the other hand, when talking together with four of the features editors at the *Tribune*, they agreed that the section has been a "pioneer in diversity." Denise Joyce, who supervised the launch of "Woman News," said previous editors had always made an effort to get minority women as models for the fashion cover. They also pointed to the ways in which other cultures and countries were covered, though this happened most often during the first few years of "Woman News," when it had a more national and international focus.

Clearly journalists find it difficult to determine what is and is not "women's news." This chapter has illustrated the various ways those working in the newsroom attempt to construct content boundaries for the women's pages. But what ultimately is illustrated in this chapter is just how fluid the boundaries of newspaper sections really are. The chapter also shows how stereotypical notions of women appear in these women's section even when the editors are trying to avoid such a picture of women. But not all in the newsroom worry about stereotyping women, and some are unapologetic about the "real" differences they perceive between men and women. The next chapter looks at some of the problems journalists have with these contemporary women's pages.

Chapter 6
Contemporary Complaints and Contradictions

Many of those interviewed in each of the three newsrooms with women's pages felt skeptical of, or conflicted about having a women's section. The skeptics, however, did not stop the news organization from moving forward with plans to designate news for women. And in many cases, editors and reporters said they eventually came around to supporting the sections, often believing that the content in these special sections was important and would not otherwise be published. Others continued to disagree with the newspaper editor's decision to offer a section of content specifically targeting women yet complied with their editors' demands, clearly a practical decision made in order to stay employed. Those news workers who had problems with these new women's pages offered familiar complaints reminiscent of those directed at traditional women's pages. They described them as marginalizing women's concerns, indicating that the content was of no interest to men, and a "dumping ground" for anything related to women. In relation to these ideas some of my participants brought up feminism. Notions of feminism in association to contemporary women's pages, however, were interesting and more complex than one might think. The ideals of feminism were both used to criticize and describe the sections.

Not only were the newly formed women's pages sometimes seem as a problem within the newsroom, many of my participants told stories of women readers who had complained about them. From my conversations however, it seemed that a higher number of readers had welcomed these contemporary sections. Whether or not the sections were embraced, most of those in the newsroom understood that the section was a marketing device meant to attract women readers who were an essential demographic for advertisers.

Same Old Solution, Same Old Problems

Among those most vocal about their disagreement with publishing a special section for women was Mary Elson, an assistant features editor at the *Chicago Tribune* and an assistant editor of "Woman News" during its launch. She explained: "The problem with all of this is I never agreed with it and I still don't. . . . It automatically diminishes the subject by putting it in the section. . . . It suggests that these are women's concerns and men don't have to pay attention" (Elson 2002). Elson's problem with a contemporary women's section mimics a key criticism of the traditional women's pages: they marginalize topics that are important to women. Elson says she was not the only one in the newsroom who expressed dissatisfaction with the *Tribune*'s decision to move forward with "Woman News." Barbara Brotman, who in 2002 had worked at the *Tribune* for twenty-three years as a reporter, feature writer, and columnist, started writing a column of personal essays about family for "Woman News" in 1994. Brotman's column originally appeared in a general features section before being moved to "Woman News." When asked how she felt about the relocation, her explanation recalled the critiques launched at the original women's pages but she said she eventually came to support the section. She explained, "I had mixed feelings about it at first because I didn't want to be ghettoized. I had mixed feelings about whether there should even be a women's news section. I think that everyone who's worked for it and edited it has had, has struggled with that whole question, but I think a lot of us feel that these are stories that wouldn't appear in the paper otherwise" (Brotman 2002). Later in our interview Brotman makes clearer her conflicted feelings about designating pages for women. After explaining, "most of the rest of the paper is man's news because much of the world is man's news," Brotman concluded the interview by saying: "I still think that this is an important section to exist and my early feelings of cynicism have faded a little bit, not a lot" (Brotman 2002).

Launching "You" editor Paula Anderson also noted her initial resistance and eventual support. But that support, like Brotman's never seemed wholehearted. For example, Anderson said: "There was always a little discomfort with the whole notion of a section that you said, 'Hey, this is for women.' I think the discomfort came from all of us to some degree, although I sort of became a convert after awhile" (Anderson 2002). *Capital Times'* features editor Bergin clearly did not support the launch of "Savvy." When I talked to her she seemed to have accepted the section but seemed relieved that she did not have to play an active role in its construction. She said: "I've not been closely involved with it from the start. At the start, because I wasn't a big fan of it and I had a hard time buying into it, and now it runs fine" (Bergin 2001). While Bergin never explicitly said so, her answers and lack of enthusiasm for the section made it fairly clear that she still does not fully support the idea of creating and publishing a separate section for women. Bergin said that when the idea of having a women's section was proposed "women in the newsroom were far from supportive of it because we have our own stereotypes of what [women's news] means and wanted to think we were further along than that—that there was no need to segregate news and content that way" (Bergin 2001).

At *The Capital Times*, Savvy's editor drew attention to another familiar criticism of traditional women's sections: that women's sections get treated like a dumping ground for any story about a woman or women. Main reporter Carr-Elsing also said "Savvy" gets treated like a "dumping ground" but illustrated less frustration than Mertz. Carr-Elsing believes that coworkers throughout the news-room simply joke about "Savvy" being a dumping ground for women's news and that it should not be taken as offensive. Mertz offered an example of how the "dumping" into "Savvy" happens:

> For example, if Dave [the editor] doesn't want something going into city or into the news section, they'll have it as a feature, because the feature section is viewed as where you can get things covered without having to use precious news space. And I think in 'Savvy' specifically, people will say, 'We don't know where to put this, let's put it in "Savvy." ' Just because you're a woman doesn't mean other women in the community will be interested in what you have to say. (Mertz 2001)

Offering another example she explained, "One other person or place that things will come from that drives me nuts is our books editor, who will say, 'Oh, this book's written by a woman.' And she gives me a stack of books written by women for women—that's not enough for me. It's got to have some sort of theme that's relevant, it's local, or be of major importance. I can't just go off the fact a woman wrote the book therefore it's interesting" (Mertz 2001). This example from Mertz highlights the danger of designating a section for women. If the books editor at *The Capital Times* uses gender as one way to reduce which books she will feature in her section then suddenly most (or all) of the books written about in the books section are by men. Not only are female authors marginalized, they are symboli-cally erased. While this is one example at one newspaper, imagine the implica-tions if women's pages existed at all newspapers in the United States. Would this type of dumping happen in other places? Not only could this sort of designation for women authors limit who reads them, it could decrease sales and ultimately result in a lesser economic gain for women authors.

As for what "Savvy's" current editor ultimately thinks about maintaining a women's section, most telling may be what she said when, without prompting, she interrupted her work, looked up at me and said, "I haven't decided if I like the women's section. I go back and forth. I'm afraid everyone will just dump stuff into that section . . . but because it is my job, I do it" (Mertz 2001). When asked what he thought of having a women's section in the newspaper, current assistant features editor at the *Lexington Herald-Leader*, Kelly Patrick, who at one time edited the "You" section, echoed the skepticism heard at the other two papers. His view also highlighted the exclusionary nature of a women's section. He said, "I think that content is good to have in there. I guess, you know, I'm resistant to the idea [of a separate section] and I think we do some of this creating sections that are so themed that it says to somebody, don't look in this section" (Patrick 2002). Patrick went on to explain that he believed some topics are of greater interest to women than men and that content needs to be in newspapers. What he does not support is labeling that content for women. Jill Williams, a senior editor of daily features at the Milwaukee paper, also acknowledged that women's interests are sometimes different from men's but said she disagreed with naming content for women. She said, "I think what makes you feel a little bit offended is that there's this implication . . . that it's limiting to women. I have problems, sometimes, when I see sections called 'women's news,' you know, and that kind of bugs me because I'm interested in the whole newspaper and I think a lot of my friends are" (Williams 2002). These points highlight a fundamental dilemma in establishing women's pages—the complex relationship between content and how that content is labeled. While most of those I interviewed seemed to agree that the content found on women's pages is important, disagreement over whether or not to label or segregate it remains. Those in favor of the strategy believe the separation makes it easier for women to find content they are interested in.

But many of those I talked to felt conflicted about the issue. "Savvy's" new and only male writer, Bill Dunn offered this perspective. When asked if he thought that having a women's section was a good idea, he answered, "yes" but only after looking toward Mertz and illustrating a bit of discomfort with the question. My interview with Dunn was the only one conducted in the newsroom and Dunn was obviously aware of the close proximity of his editors. He did elaborate, though: "I think it can be overdone, [but] one day a week is certainly not too much" (Dunn 2001). Later when he talked about his concern over gender stereotypes in the section, he clearly illustrated his skepticism in having a section for women. To explain why he felt it was problematic to designate topics by sex or gender, he said: "There's a perception that relationships are more interesting to women but that's not the case with me. It may have been in the past but I think that's changed" (Dunn 2001).

Those staff who expressed opposition to women's sections at *The Capital Times*' offered relatively mild complaints compared with a current copy editor, Judy Ettenhofer, who worked as assistant city editor when "Savvy" first appeared. As a woman in the newsroom, she said: "My concern was it would be too fluffy and I didn't want to be a party to 'let's write about hair, makeup, and fashion' " (Ettenhofer 2001). Ettenhofer believes "Savvy" is "hit or miss. We do some really good things but also we don't go deep enough. The stories are not as deep and substantive as I'd like to see" (Ettenhofer 2001). She remembers the original "Savvy" editor wanting to have a more substantive section but struggling with resources. This complaint about a lack of resources is reminiscent of the traditional women's pages and even the newly named style or feature sections that began publishing in the 1970s.

"Woman News" editor Navratil offered an alternative and optimistic perspective to the common complaints that women's pages were dumping grounds that ghettoize any story or issue related to women. She explained:

> I've heard that a lot and part of what I would say is that a lot of times the story does come to us and if we do think it is a bigger story we do pass it on to news or let them know and find out whether they'll be able to do something and negotiate. Having

a women's section keeps people aware. It's almost that we're a watch dog to make sure some of this stuff gets covered and if it doesn't look like it's going to get covered in news or couldn't be the kind of story or length of story or depth of story that we can do in 'Woman News' then that's where we can do it. (Navratil 2002)

Navratil's comment presents a positive reaction to an old argument regarding the benefits of women's pages. It also reinforces the point illustrated in chapter four about the reason why many who worked for women's pages did not oppose them. In other words, women's pages were necessary because they offered news that would not otherwise make it into the newspaper. Further, it highlights the belief that "women's issues" have failed to be integrated into all areas of the newspaper.

Feminism and Contemporary Women's Pages

While I was interested in understanding how feminist ideologies might play into the conceptualization and construction of contemporary women's pages, I was hesitant to bring this up explicitly during my interviews. Rather I was interested in seeing if and how feminism was brought up and discussed by my interview participants. The manner in which feminism came into the conversations were at times predictable but always were informative about both how the pages and feminism were perceived, and what influence feminism, as a social movement and ideological perspective, has had on contemporary women's pages.

Navratil, the current "Woman News" editor, made it clear that her section did not espouse a feminist political view but instead presented a variety of women's perspectives, including those from the Christian Right. In other words, she acknowledged that while readers may view some content as supportive of a feminist perspective, certainly other stories could not be interpreted that way. But Janet Franz, one of the *Tribune*'s editors who helped supervise the launch of "Woman News," believes editors would not have created the section without feminism and the women's movement. She said: "I don't know that it would exist if there hadn't been some sort of realization that women have a certain set of needs that maybe men don't" (Franz 2002). The comment was particularly ironic in light of the comment earlier in which feminism was noted as a major cause for the termination of women's pages in the 1970s. Franz, however, was not the only editor at the *Tribune* who believed feminism had been an impetus in the creation of "Woman News." Denise Joyce agreed, remembering the original "Woman's News" as "kind of harder edged. That was the strident tone; it was really kind of up there and in your face." Franz described editors as spending "a lot on development of legislation for women, things going on with this person, what they'd done for different causes." Geoff Brown, associate managing editor of features, agreed with Franz, Rudolph, and Joyce about the historical relationship between "Woman News" and feminism but said now feminism surfaces only as news. He explained, "Just like Janet said there wouldn't be one without that movement. And do they have any affect on it now? Only as newsmakers, period. I don't think that anyone of you six years ago sat there thinking about how can we make this more militant to satisfy that contingent of people. I think that never happened it's just all in the mix" (Brown 2002). The four editors explained how the section changed over time. What had been a section targeting a syndication market and covering international and national issues, began to focus more on Chicago women. Much of this had to do with "hard facts" about the failed attempt at syndication of the section. Janet Franz took over the section at that time (1999) and said "the goal when I took over was to make it more readable and reader friendly to the people here rather than to try to draw these stories that were sort of marginal elsewhere" (Franz 2002). Joyce added: "I think before [Franz] came in we were doing the stories about the plight of India, the plight of women in Africa, the plight of women . . . ." While the editors talked with pride about the types of stories found in the early years of "Woman News" they said it suffered from being the same from issue to issue and was often criticized as being a "downer of a section" (Franz 2002). This illustrates the struggle women's section editors are caught in. On the one hand, editors may want to provide serious news as not to demean the interests of women. On the other hand, these sections are typically understood to be feature sections (or "soft" news) and are areas of the newspaper where readers turn for lighter content.

The words "feminism" and the "women's movement"—and notions related to them—most often came up in interviews at *The Capital Times* and the least often at the *Lexington Herald-Leader* where current editors certainly did not see the "You" section as presenting a feminist ideology. Possibly because the recent editors of the section consider the section more about family than for women, no one talked about feminism's current influence on the content. When words and notions related to feminism and the women's movement were mentioned in interviews, it was most often in relation to feminism's influence on the elimination of past women's sections. For example, "Savvy's" lead writer Carr-Elsing said, "The days of the old women's sections, you know, when you talked about the garden club and who was wearing what and who came in with who, you know, have long been shed by the wayside. Women's sections, I think, you know, had their heyday and they kind of went out of vogue with the feminist movement—maybe with the early '70s" (Carr-Elsing 2001). This is especially interesting in the context of the *Tribune* editor's believing that feminism can be credited with the creation of their paper's contemporary women's section. But then again, Carr-Elsing is distinguishing between the traditional women's pages and the contemporary women's section she helps to create. After Carr-Elsing brought up the feminist movement, I asked if she identified herself as a feminist. She explained: "Sure. But feminist just because I believe in promoting women's causes and women's issues."

Mertz, "Savvy's" editor in 2001, possessed a clear feminist consciousness that is evident in both her work and her educational background even though it was neither always apparent, nor without contradictions. On the first day I spent at *The Capital Times*, I discovered Mertz in the middle of a telephone interview with one of the authors of "Manifesta: Young Women, Feminism and the Future." The authors were in town for a reading and book signing. The choice to cover the event illustrated her interest in including feminist content in "Savvy." She was writing a feature story on the authors. *The Capital Times* had hired Mertz to take over its women's section less than two years before my interview with her. Bergin, the features editor who was in charge of interviewing candidates for the position, says it is not a coincidence that Mertz holds a women's studies degree along with her journalism degree from the University of Wisconsin, Madison. Bergin explained: "there were other finalists [for the position], but there was no one else who had that [women's studies degree] component, which I felt was important" (Bergin 2001). Mertz further emphasized the relevance and importance of her women's studies degree. Taking an editing position appealed to Mertz, she said, because "I was trying to use my women's studies degree in some way and I felt I couldn't do that in a reporter position—I'd need some more room to work" (Mertz 2001). When asked exactly how her specialized degree applied, she explained: "It gives me a ton of ideas—ideas for stories built off theories. I understand a women's studies perspective of what women have gone through" (Mertz 2001). Mertz offered some previously published "Savvy" stories as examples of how she believed her background in feminist studies informs her work. Among them:

- An article about how stereotypes in the music industry affect women and the musical instruments they play, which she said had been a topic in one of her classes;
- A story focusing on a single mom going back into the workforce, an issue she said "lots of women's studies classes dealt with";
- An article on how beauty images and the cosmetic industry negatively affect women; and
- A story about Tupperware-like sex-toy parties that Mertz called "an example of a lighter story" framed in feminist terms—"it tells about our sexual liberation and freedom" (Mertz 2001).

But while Mertz could quickly offer a handful of stories that she felt supported a feminist perspective, a glance at a few weeks worth of "Savvy" reveals as much content that feminist critics would argue presented women's interests as stereotypical or trivial, for example, relationship and advice columns and stories about fashion.

Readers and Colleagues React

I did not interview readers of newspapers or reporters outside of women's pages and features departments yet a number of my interview participants talked about how their readers and newsroom colleagues had responded to these sex-specific sections. The reactions were mixed. At the *Chicago Tribune*, Joyce said, "I remember in one of the focus groups, I can't remember if a man said this or a woman, but they would say that the men in the household would read it because they wanted to be clued in to what the women in their life were thinking." Franz, however, explained how at the *Tribune* readers also expressed concern with designating content by gender and marginalizing women's concerns. Franz, who oversaw the start of "Woman News" at the *Tribune*, talked about one letter the paper received. She explained that it was "a very long letter about how just annoyed and horrified she was with the whole idea of it and how her friends thought it was just a terrible thing and how could the *Tribune* put all these women in this section and just act like it was fifty years ago or something like that. And women should be through the entire paper and we're people just like everybody else. And I saw the point, I thought there were points there that were reasonable and I could understand" (Franz 2002). Mike Johnson, the *Herald-Leader*'s deputy managing editor's recollection offered evidence that some readers noted the exclusionary nature of "You" as well. He said he remembers getting comments from men who said they were interested in the content and asked why the section claimed to offer "News for Today's Women." Anderson also noted the backlash from readers as well as coworkers. She explained: "We took a lot of heat in our own newsroom over it, by reporters and editors who thought it was silly and frivolous and that we were underestimating the intellect of women" (Anderson 2002).

Ettenhofer, a *Capital Times'* copy editor in 2001 who worked as assistant city editor when "Savvy" first appeared, acknowledged the difficulty in reflecting back, but said she and other women in the newsroom were uncomfortable with the idea and asked management to hold focus groups before moving forward. Unfortunately no one in the newsroom was able to locate the focus group report and the woman who conducted the research said in 2001 that she no longer had a copy of her findings. The researcher did say, however, that she remembers women participants not being enthusiastic about the idea of a special section in the newspaper. The paper's current editor in chief, Dave Zweifel, recalls, "the research was really supportive of this idea of doing something, having a special section for women" (Zweifel 2001). Conversely, Ettenhofer said about the focus groups, "I was struck with the number of women who thought they would be offended" (Ettenhofer 2001). During my interviews at each of the papers, however, I was told by at least one person how popular the women's pages were at these newspapers. Carr-Elsing said her sources are usually thrilled to be in the section because they are regular readers of it. Mertz believed the section gained respect after people became familiar with it. She, however, pointed to something others I interviewed had also mentioned: the reaction inside the newsroom. She explained, "I [get] the impression that when it first came out, people thought it would be like the old school fashion section, it was going to be society news, who was at the tea party last week. I think that gradually they've learned that it can be a place where there can be interesting and meaningful dialogues about issues and I think the general public knows that. They've probably embraced it more than people in our own newsroom, because we have time to analyze it. We overanalyze it" (Mertz 2001).

Making Women Special, Making Advertisers Happy

Regardless of how those in the newsrooms I interviewed felt about creating special sections for women, there was little debate about one point: why it was part of their newspaper. Throughout conversations with the publishers, editors, and reporters of special women's sections it became clear that contemporary women's pages had been created as a marketing device to entice and satisfy advertisers. Like the original women's sections more than a century earlier, these new sections were not created out of a concern for women readers. Anyway, that was never the underlying reason.

The Capital Times' publisher explained research indicated women were a key market newspapers needed to reach. This he said justified the section. But, he said, "I think you could go to one lectern and make a case that it's the right thing to do and go to the other one and make the case that it's a marketing opportunity" (Frink 2001). Dave Zweifel, the editor in chief at *The Capital Times*, said the importance of women readers was talked about at conferences and meetings he attended with other editors and publishers. He said: "We spread information about each other's markets, it became pretty apparent that we needed to do something to reach out to women. Researchers were telling us that women were making the decision whether to buy a newspaper or not" (Zweifel 2001). This understanding of marketing strategy was not something that only those in the top decision-making positions were clear about. I asked Carr-Elsing, the reporter for "Savvy," if she thought the section began "because women weren't finding these stories in other parts of the paper?" She answered: "Yes and also I think it was a marketing decision because women had the dollars to spend." At the *Chicago Tribune* the marketing reality of the section was particularly evident in the types of content it originally carried, according to more than one of the people I interviewed there. That is, the section was filled with national and international news so that it could be sold to papers across the country. Clearly, then, this section was constructed as a money making endeavor.

As this chapter illustrates, not all of those working in newsrooms producing contemporary women's pages embraced these new sex-specific pages. The next chapter offers viewpoints from within two newsrooms where journalists were not creating explicitly named sections for women. What will become evident in the next chapter, however, is just how prevalent the concern for women reader is in the newspaper industry.

Chapter 7
Resistance, Reason, and Real Change

Two of the newspapers where I visited did not have explicitly named women's pages. I wanted to get a perspective from feature section editors and writers who were not involved in the production of these contemporary women's pages but instead were creating feature-style content meant for a general audience. The perspectives of these news workers were interesting, particularly because most were familiar with the contemporary women's pages at either *The Capital Times* and/or *Chicago Tribune*. Those I talked to who worked at the *Milwaukee Journal Sentinel* and *Wisconsin State Journal* for the most part expressed satisfaction and relief in being able to construct a gender/sex neutral features section. Even so, many of those who were not working on sex-specific women's pages understood why they might be important. In fact, throughout my interviews at each of the newspapers I discovered journalists who justified these women-targeted pages. They believed that women's pages were needed because the idea of integrating women's interests and bylines into all areas of the newspaper had failed. And, they explained, newspapers still need women readers. This, however, begs the question: Have these women's pages actually brought women back to newspapers? The *Lexington Herald-Leader*—and those I talked to there—offer the best answer to this question, as this chapter will show. As a whole, the interviews from each of the newsrooms offer one other important point and stand together as a strong argument for diversifying newsroom staff. During my interviews at all five newspapers journalists talked about how individual reporters and editors shape the news through their understandings, lived experiences, and perspectives. With this in mind, it seems natural that the more diversity in the newsroom, the more variety in news content.

Resisting Women's Sections

The inclusion of the *Milwaukee Journal Sentinel* proved to be an especially in-teresting case for this book. While it was chosen for inclusion in this book because it did not publish pages targeting women, during the interview period I discovered that the top feature section editors were actually in the midst of designing such pages. Top editors at the newspaper were pushing for "women's pages," according to assistant managing editor for features Diana Bacha. Bacha, however, along with assistant entertainment and features editor, Jim Higgins, firmly disagreed with explicitly naming pages for women and narrowing news content by sex. So while a two-page prototype had been developed for women readers and the page would be published in the Sunday features section, the pages would be titled "Compass" without any reference to a target audience. It was a small victory for Bacha and Higgins, who were forced to create the pages with women in mind but felt some satisfaction in their ability to resist a title that indicated sex-specific content. Neither Bacha nor Higgins had a problem with the content; what they had a problem with was reinforcing stereotypical notions of men and women's interests. Even if more women may be interested in the content of these new "Compass" pages, without the sex-specific designation, the two editors felt the content was open and inviting to all of their readers.

Bacha said she turned to women's magazines when developing the prototype, as editors of the original women's pages had done more than a century earlier. Among those magazines piled in a box in Bacha's office: *Shape*, *Glamour*, and *Ms.* (at the time an advertising-free feminist magazine). Bacha, who said she welcomed talking about contemporary women's pages because it acknowledges a real dilemma for newspapers, explained that the resistance to naming a section for women had both personal and organizational components. A main part of the organizational reasoning has to do with the fact that the *Journal Sentinel* does not have a daily features section. This means more limited space for feature stories, and Bacha sees women's pages as too limiting and exclusionary. Bacha's personal opposition to women's pages echoed past criticisms of women's pages. Her explanation also illustrated her understanding of the history of women's pages and her struggles with conflicting personal and organizational ideologies. She explained:

> So once you start calling that section a women's section, you've lost all of that [space]. The second part is that—it isn't so much an internal issues, it's more of a personal philosophy—is that I don't like ghettoizing, the whole ghettoizing women's topics. I just want to be passed that. You know, I really can sympathize with the fact that we still need some women's sections, but I don't want a daily newspaper to be doing that. I'd rather be inclusive. I'd rather, you know, we are a broadcast medium; we are a community-based medium. We're not a niche publication and I'd rather see us putting on a section that is more inclusive and say, listen, if there are family issues, we all have families, you know, . . . I think the topics we would write for a women's section are interesting to many different people. So we're choosing to create, in this case, really just two pages right now that will include topics that are of great interest to women and that's our first audience, but that will not exclude men. (Bacha 2002)

Higgins had coined the phrase "A section for women and people who like them" as a way to define in-house what type of content the new pages will include. When asked "Why not just call 'Compass' a women's section?" Higgins resisted the notion that content could be categorized by sex in any absolute manner. He responded by asking "But why? My answer to that is why artificially label it? There's no particular, I don't think there's any special marketing value to putting that name on it and why exclude the men" (Higgins 2002). He also noted the marginalizing and stigmatizing effect a sex-specific name might have on news content. He said, "There's a way in which it would be demeaning to say, OK, the inside two pages are women's news, you know, and the rest, you're almost making a statement about the rest of the paper: 'Well, women, they're not even important enough to get a cover' " (Higgins 2002). Bacha, who also believed the same problems occurred when sections were named for women, went a step further in her criticism with sex targeted content. She addressed the fact that newsrooms are still, for the most part, male dominated. She explained, "I also think there's a weird thing that happens in newsrooms that are still very male-oriented and when they hear women's section, they diminish it. It just happens. And I don't have enough faith that by putting the label 'women' in our section, it won't get that stigma again. You know, I think it takes an unusual set of circumstances for that not to happen in the newsroom" (Bacha 2002). Bacha did say, however, that she can't be that critical of other newspaper editors who have instituted contemporary women's pages since newspapers have "earned this problem" of having fewer women readers. And she understands the organizational pressures that affect content. Others at the *Journal Sentinel* that I interviewed had little to say about the topic and seemed to have given it little thought, as they were not in decision-making positions in the newsroom or had not been involved in the discussion and creation of "Compass."

At the *State Journal*, themed sections are published each day of the week, and editor Chris Juzwik said his main goal is to offer diversity and a surprise to his readers. But because of the broad labels given to the daily feature sections, Juzwik said there are not boundaries or clear definitions for the types of stories and topics on his pages. He explained: "I'm one who doesn't really like labels or tags or anything like that and so I tend to rebel against those kinds of things more than others might. I will take any story and turn it into a feature story" (Juzwik 2002). This perspective echoes my earlier discussions about the precarious differences between news and feature sections and what constitutes a news story versus a feature story. Juzwik said he and his staff consider a diverse readership but that he is more interested in those who do not read the newspaper's features sections than those who do. Who he expressed an interest in reaching were young readers, something more and more newspaper publishers and editors are thinking about. He said he continually tries to think of ways to bring younger readers into the paper. When asked specifically if he thought "women's news" existed, he brought up the *Tribune*'s "Woman News" section and also the problems with naming content for women and therefore excluding men. But his answer was complex and contradictory as he fully supported the *Tribune*'s section and described it as non-exclusionary. What was clear, however, was his relief in not having to designate content by sex or gender. He explained, "Sure. I'm sure there are more, that there are topics that women are more interested in than men, but I would hate to.... I don't like the boxes and fences. I would hate to say that, you know, that this story would not be of interest to men" (Juzwik 2002). Further, while Juzwik believed that the *Tribune* created quality women's pages, his critique of *The Capital Times'* "Savvy" was less than favorable. It is only fair to point out, however, that Savvy is constructed with considerably fewer resources than "Woman News." This he acknowledged. Juzwik also noted that women were an important "niche" market. This point about niche markets is interesting in light of Bacha's comments about the *Milwaukee Journal Sentinel* and her strong belief that newspapers should be for a general audience and not target niche markets. But as is evidenced by the history of women's sections, newspapers have considered women an important niche market for more than a century.

All of those I talked to at the *Milwaukee Journal Sentinel* and Wisconsin *State Journal* said that feature sections were constructed with both men and women readers in mind. Sandy Kallio, an assistant features editor at the *State Journal*, who has worked for the paper for more than twenty years, believed there had been a gradual change in thinking about feature section audiences. She said, twenty years ago it was much more of a women's section even though none of the pages carried that title. She explained, " I mean, it was. I think that was the audience we all had in mind" (Kallio 2002). This highlights the multitude of contradictions surrounding the switch from women's to style pages and even the contemporary women's pages. As I illustrated earlier in the book, even though most newspapers stopped publishing "women's pages" in the 1970s, many remained women's pages in the minds of editors and reporters. They were simply renamed. Also, a number of those I interviewed who produce the contemporary women's pages (or read them as Juzwik said) believe they are for men and women. This represents another contradiction. It brings up the same underlying confusion and begs the same questions about why to name the section for women if the audience really is broader.

Frank Denton, the editor of the *State Journal* since 1986, exhibited a depth of thinking about feature sections and their relationship to women readers. In fact, even though his paper did not publish contemporary women's pages, his knowl-·edge of the history and current debate about women's sections was among the deepest of any person interviewed for this book. This knowledge can be credited to both his long career, a doctoral education in newspaper management, and having worked as the assistant women's section editor in Detroit in 1976, where he worked under Scott McGhee (the same person who had created the prototype for the *Lexington Herald-Leader's* contemporary women's section). Denton believes contemporary women's pages, which balance the diverse aspects of women, have a place in U.S. newspapers. And while the *State Journal* does not currently offer pages explicitly targeting women readers, he said he is not against—and has even recently considered—women's pages in his newspaper. At the time, however, there were no plans to move forward with a women's section in the *State Journal*. Instead Denton's current focus echoed Juzwik's concern for attracting young readers.

Rethinking Women's News

At the time of my visit, the *Herald-Leader* editors were only days away from launching a thematic set of new feature sections and "You" would not be included. In 2002, the *Tribune* editors had also recently restructured their feature offerings. The change meant a switch from Sunday to Wednesday for "Woman News" and, maybe more significantly, "Woman News" at the top of the section became simply "WN." The explanation for this nameplate switch varied. Some editors said the revision happened simply because with the new typeface "Woman News" would not fit. Others, however, said the goal was to downplay that the pages were constructed for women. These changes might also be explained by the industry's heightened focus on gaining young readers. As the 1990s drew to an end, newspaper industry leaders in large part turned their attention away from a declining female readership and toward a nonreading younger population. Ironically and surprising, *Lexington Herald-Leader* publisher Tim Kelly said to create pages targeting teens would not be the answer to his paper's new "at-risk" reading audience. The reason: the solution would be offensive and exclusionary. He explained that "the worst things that you could do is develop a section that is just for teens or a page that's just for teens, because basically what it does, it just kind of compartmentalizes that in saying, 'OK, once a month we're going to, you know, throw this to you' " (Kelly 2002). His answer seemed perplexing and reminded me of what the editor of "Savvy" had said about targeting minorities. Both of these editors believed it was acceptable to designate a section for women yet unacceptable for other groups.

The elimination of the *Lexington Herald-Leader*'s "You" section offers evidence of the paper's altered focus. But the decision to stop publishing "You"—and even an earlier decision to change the focus to family rather than women—made sense for the *Lexington Herald-Leader*. By 2002 the newspaper boasted a higher female than male readership. Publisher Kelly explained in 2002 that the readership polls for his newspaper showed a "read yesterday" split of 48 percent male and 52 percent female. In the early 1990s when the editors launched "You" those numbers were 57 percent male and 43 percent female. But Kelly, along with other editors in the newsroom, said "You" gets credit for only a small part of the readership change. Deputy managing editor Johnson said, "I think the 'You' section we learned a lot from and I think it sharpened our sense in certain ways about trying to think of women readers and that type of thing, but you know, I think the best way to reach any kind of group is throughout the entire newspaper" (Johnson 2002). Other in the newsroom echoed Johnson's belief that "You" had gotten editors and reporters in the newsroom thinking about women. This change in readership demographics at the *Herald-Leader* that occurred over a ten-year period only happened after management at the newspaper made some significant and calculated decisions. Evidence of this heightened awareness of women readers and desire to make sure women find themselves represented throughout the entire newspaper came out during the daily news meetings observed at the *Herald-Leader*. For example, as editors and designers planned the next day's front page, which was during the 2002 Olympics, the staff decided on a centerpiece photograph of women's figure skating because they believed it would appeal to more women as well as put a woman's face on the front page.

Another significant change made at the *Herald-Leader* during the 1990s, which editors agreed made the most difference in changing newspaper content and the readership numbers, had been the addition of women in newsroom decision-making positions. Publisher Tim Kelly explained how when he took over in 1996 there were five people reporting to the publisher and none of them were women. Now he says of the five people who report to him, three are women: the senior vice president for sales and marketing, the chief executive officer, and the editor. He went on to explain that he has a ten-member executive committee made up of five men and five women, that the editorial page editor is an African-American woman, and that one of the assistant managing editors is a woman. And, he said, "We've got a male in the traditional role of features editor" (Kelly 2002).

At Madison's *Capital Times*, publisher Clayton Frink had no plans to dissolve the women's pages when I interviewed him, though "Savvy's" editor said she has seen a constant decrease in space and resources during her short tenure. As an afternoon daily in a two-newspaper town, Frink said his paper does not have a lot to lose by experimenting with contemporary women's pages. But he said he honestly does not know if "Savvy" has attracted more women readers or kept them reading his paper. In fact, about having women's pages, Frink said, "I'm not even sure it's correct" (Frink 2001). The readership studies still show more men than women reading his paper. As for the *Chicago Tribune*'s "Woman News," on more than one occasion during my interviews different editors said the section is in constant danger of being dissolved. The "Woman News" editor explained, "It's always been a fight for life, fight for survival with the section and from what I understand is that every time it's come up for another round of the firing squad readers have come up with such loyal intensity about the section. . . . Somehow it's managed to hold on and again even this year with the economy so bad it's been a little bit of a worry" (Navratil 2002). She went on to explain why she believed readers felt so devoted to the section, saying "I think the reason our readers are so loyal is that it's a voice of women, it's always for women and it's personal and it speaks to them in a way the rest of the paper really doesn't" (Navratil 2002). Apparently the section does not bring in significant advertising revenue and this is a partial explanation for why the section was recently moved from Sunday to Wednesday—advertising is less costly during the weekdays. Consensus of those

I interviewed in the newsroom, however, was that the section remains in publication simply because of its intense popularity, even though it is not believed to have a major impact on female readership figures. This conflict between the popularity of a section, its production costs, and capacity to bring in revenue is an interesting one in light of gender news content preferences. Sports pages are one of the costliest sections for most daily newspapers yet earn little revenue to counter that cost. But many argue because sports sections are especially popular with male readers, newspapers will not consider eliminating them. On the other hand, the popularity of the women's sections in Madison and Chicago has not stopped editors at those newspapers from downsizing and considering eliminating them.

An Editor's Influence: The Shaping and Reshaping of Women's News

At each of the five newspapers I visited, I asked those who worked on the women's pages or feature sections to talk about how the pages were constructed. With my questions I hoped to get at who conceptualized these sections and who ultimately shaped the content. Publishers, editors, and reporters pointed primarily to individuals as those who construct and conceptualize contemporary women's sections. They explained that it was the editor of the section that had control over the end product, but that reporters had a lot of say in what stories they chose to write. For example, Carr-Elsing, lead writer for "Savvy," said she believed her interests as a parent inspired many story ideas. She explained, "My daughter was quite old and still using a pacifier so I talked to pediatricians about, you know, is that harmful for a four-year-old to have a pacifier in her mouth? Is she going to have teeth problems? [Ideas come from] things that I would confront and my friends. You know, I would see things going on in their homes or their lives or they would have questions and I'd think, 'whoa, that's something I could do a story about and share that information" (Carr-Elsing 2001). This idea of a person's identities influencing news came up often. Another example comes from my conversation with Paula Anderson at the *Lexington Herald-Leader*. She had mentioned that the current editor of the paper was a woman. Asked if it makes a differences, she responded:

> Absolutely it makes a difference. It also makes a difference when your city editor is a woman. It makes a difference when your editorial page editor is a woman. . . . I can look at the features section today and say there's a difference in having a female features editor and a male features editor. It's not to say one's better than the other. There's just a difference in sort of your story line a little bit. I think that it's the same when you have minorities in key leadership positions. It helps you think a little bit differently and just raises those issues to the table. (Anderson 2002)

My interview participants offered insight into how editors influence content, particularly noting how the contemporary women's pages I examined changed with each new editor of the section. Mertz, "Savvy's" editor, is given full credit by others in the newsroom for the content in her section. All of her senior editors agreed that Mertz shapes "Savvy." Likewise, at the *Tribune* and the *Lexington Herald-Leader*, senior editors point to editors of "Woman News" and "You" for primarily conceptualizing and constructing the latest iterations of the sections. They say it is because the women's page editors at each of these newspapers assign stories and help reporters to shape the content. And I heard often, senior-level editors offer little input in the construction of women's pages. This is a reality reminiscent of past women's sections, when women editors were free to create their pages without male editors looking over their shoulders. But while women's page editors at each of the newspapers are given credit for shaping their sections, each said that many of the story ideas come from their reporters. As editors, they explained, they sometimes offer little feedback about the stories reporters write for the section.

Mertz said her reporters each have their ideas of what they want to work on and she welcomes the story diversity. But even Mertz noted the control and relative autonomy section editors have. Navratil, the current "Woman News" editor, also acknowledged an editor's influence on a section but pointed out that the uniqueness of a feature's section targeting women translates into more shaping by the editor. She explained, "I think the section—more than a lot of other sections—really reflects its editor and its editor's priorities and their personal lives because it's a personal section. So, by nature of that it's just natural that if the editor is a mother or is younger, you're going to see some of that creep into what we cover" (Navratil 2002). Editor's influences are also illustrated in the fact that "You" and *The Capital Times'* "Savvy" originally targeted working mothers and the sections contained numerous stories about parenting and juggling work with motherhood. Conversely, the *Tribune*'s "Woman News" carried nothing about children. "Woman News" columnist Barbara Brotman said the decision was very deliberate but believes the section ended up slighting women's realities. She explained, "This was about women in the work world and political world; this was not about mommies and babies. As the years passed different editors came in and I think there was a feeling of we were leaving something out that was important to women's lives, we were slighting something" (Brotman 2002). Parenting stories eventually began appearing in "Woman News." But by the time Navratil took over "Woman News" a new family and relationships section had been added to the *Tribune*'s weekly features offerings and in 2002 these topics were absent from the women's pages again. On the other hand, after a few years "You" eventually morphed into a family and relationships section and the "News for Today's Women" subtitle was abandoned in 1996.

It is telling that the changes in topics and types of stories found in "Woman News," "You," and "Savvy," editors and reporters repeatedly said, coincided with the hiring of a new editor for the section. But it is important to understand how organizational decisions and intentions shaped these changes. For example, while

"Woman News" started out offering a heavy amount of national and international news, when Jean Rudolph took over as editor in 1999 the section took on a more local voice. This, of course, was something she was hired to change indicating the change in content was influenced by more than the individual editor. She explained, "The goal was to make it more readable and reader friendly to the people here rather than to try to draw these stories that were sort of marginal elsewhere" (Rudolph 2002). It was Rudolph's responsibility to turn these goals into a reality. With the hiring of Navratil, the section turned toward more timely news and also features stories that appeal to a younger audience, her editors said. While Navratil said she wanted the section to carry serious news, the "hard" news angle can also be attributed to the new editor of the features department who is pushing all of the department's sections to offer more timely news.

At the *Herald-Leader*, Paula Anderson, the original "You" editor, described the section as morphing over time. She explained: "There was an evolution of editors in there. You know, newspapers always change when new editors come in. There's always a bit of a personality shift" (Anderson 2002). The *Herald-Leader*'s publisher Tim Kelly, who was involved in the launch of "You," echoed the point about an editor's influence on content. He said: "Probably it morphed because of the way things just evolve in any newsroom. You know, different people have access to it. We've had two or three features editors since then and several assistant editors" (Kelly 2002).

Not just new editors and personnel changes explain the transformation of these sections over time. Other explanations for the transformation of these sections include a decrease in resources, diminished excitement as the momentum of a new section drops off, and a lack of advertiser interest. As for limited resources, Mertz said space had "gotten progressively tighter over the years, and you've got to fight for what you have" (Mertz 2002). The disinterest businesses have in advertising for the section, according to the advertising manager at the *Lexington Herald-Leader* and also editors at the *Tribune*, has more to do with the placement of the women's section than the content within it. Advertisers desire to be in the front sections of newspapers or as far forward as possible. These women's sections are typically at the end of the paper. Another example of how content for women is marginalized.

An Argument for Diversity

Another point that continually came up in my interviews as a justification for women's pages, calls attention to a common and historic complaint about U.S. newspapers. That is, that they are edited by and for white men. While clearly the diversity in newsrooms has changed over the decades, those I interviewed expressed a belief that the problem still existed to a degree. In fact, this is why, I heard several times, that women's pages are still needed. For example, *Chicago Tribune* "Woman News" columnist Barbara Brotman said, "I still feel that most of the rest of the paper is man's news because much of the world is man's news." Other editors at the *Tribune* pointed out research documenting the relatively low number of female bylines and sources on the front pages of main U.S. newspapers to illustrate this point about male dominated newspapers. This argument as a justification for producing women's pages is not new but seems to give up on the idea of integrating women's concerns into all areas of the newspaper. The point, however, in conjunction with the previous section that posits the power individual women's pages editors have to shape content, offers a sound argument for diversifying newsrooms and counters beliefs that newsroom socialization erases personal differences.

This chapter has illustrated just how common the idea of contemporary women's pages might be. While I chose to visit two newspapers without explicitly named women's pages, one was grappling with the issue at the moment and the editor at the other newspaper said he had considered it for his paper. Especially interesting is how the features editors at the *Milwaukee Journal Sentinel* resisted upper-level editors requests to create explicitly named women's pages. Instead they negotiated for the creation of pages primarily for a female audience, but without the sex-specific name. These features editors believed that to label content for women would have negative effects, including marginalizing and "ghettoizing" issues of concern to women, stereotyping interests of men and women, and creating a newsroom "dumping ground" for anything related to women. This chapter also offers evidence that individual editors and reporters have agency in constructing women's pages. Using this information, I posit that diversity in the newsroom, and particularly in decision-making positions, is a strong argument for diversifying newsrooms across the country while higher-level interests may influence individual interests, personal agency does exist. In the following and final chapter, I consider the main points of the book and draw conclusions about the ways in which newspapers have constructed a female audience. In these conclusions I weigh what I have learned and argue why I believe explicitly named women's pages are not only unnecessary in contemporary times, but are offensive, and counter to women's progress inside and outside of newspapers.

Part IV

Conclusions

Chapter 8

What Is in a Name? An Argument for Integration, Not Segregation

The particular day that I interviewed staff at the *Chicago Tribune* the "Woman News" editor was preparing to publish a "late-breaking" local story about an abortion protest. She planned to place the story above the fold on the front page of her section, for it to be the lead article. Her excitement showed as she explained how her women's pages would have serious news that week rather than the typical feature stories and "fluff" associated with these sex-specific sections. This incident, however, illustrates perfectly a major problem, past and present, with designating newspaper content for one sex. In other words, it is problematic when editors designate important news as women's content rather than present it in a manner that indicates a level of importance to all readers. This positioning of news content maintains and reinforces women's marginalized status in American culture and demeans issues of interest and/or importance to women. Further, it supports an idea that women are responsible for various societal-wide issues. In essence, women's pages—contemporary or not—marginalize and "ghettoize" women's issues and become a newsroom "dumping ground" for anything slightly related to women.

This particular example at the *Tribune* demonstrates how, when women's pages exist, editors ghettoize newspaper content by relegating what should be general news to sex-specific pages. Through women's pages, editors of mainstream daily newspapers reify community-wide social issues, interests, and problems as sex-specific and in doing so subordinate them. This case at the *Tribune* is especially interesting because while often stories related to women end up on the women's pages or not in the paper at all, that was not the case here. Another editor overseeing one of the news sections of the *Tribune* had planned to publish the abortion protest story but the "Woman's News" editor got the story first. It is difficult to blame women's page editors though for the problems that stem from wanting late-breaking news in their sections. Navratil's desire to place this news story in the women's section is reminiscent of the wish women's page editors of the past had to make their sections newsworthy and relevant. Women's page editors over the years have strived to create pertinent sections for their female readers, rather than simply content that positions their sex as consumers of goods and services

103

and caretakers of families and homes.

The difficulty with trying to define news for women and the marginalization that occurs with the placement of this news is compounded by the tension women journalists have felt over the contradictory nature of these sections—both representative of opportunities in the newsroom and impediments to their advancement as journalists. They have given women the chance to define news but have also reinforced binary notions of news content based on stereotypical notions of gender. They have aided in the construction of women as consumers but, at the same time, have offered women important information otherwise absent in many daily newspapers. The contradictions and tensions surrounding explicitly named women's pages, however, do not stop here. These concepts of incongruity and disharmony sum up most aspects of these sex-specific newspaper sections. Another area where this holds true is in the relationship of these sections to feminism and the women's movement. Many credit feminism with enlightening the newspaper industry and inspiring it to eliminate these sex-specific sections in the late 1960s. At the same time, feminism has been used as a justification for re-creating these sections in the 1990s. The sections have been both embraced and criticized by journalists, feminists, and readers.

A major reason both past and present that the journalism industry has embraced, or at least considered, these sex-specific sections rests on economics. The economic environment and a concern for revenue sources played a major role in newspaper industry leaders' decisions to first establish and then reintroduce women's pages into U.S. newspapers. Newspapers, like any business, rely on revenue sources—advertisers and an audience—for survival. Publishers in the 1890s, aware of cultural shifts that transformed women into the primary shoppers in a typical household, wanted to appeal to women readers. These publishers believed that by offering specific content for women, they could bring more women readers to the paper and ultimately deliver a female audience to advertisers.

In the 1990s circumstances were similar. At the three newspapers in this study where contemporary women's pages were added, publishers, editors, and journalists said marketing concerns and a desire for more advertising revenue resulted in the decision to try women's pages. Newspaper publishers and editors, now worried about a declining female readership, hoped that designing a section of news just for women would inspire women to read their newspaper. In the 1980s and 1990s, however, industry leaders acknowledged that an absence of content of interest to women and lack of women's bylines in daily newspapers had resulted in the declining female readership. But rather than try integrating women into all sections of the newspaper, some in the industry relied on an old idea. Industry leaders looked to the past to solve a contemporary problem. And even when many in the newsroom believed creating explicitly named women's pages would only recreate past problems rather than solve the issue of a declining female readership, this "solution" went forward. The marketing possibilities were made clear in the original version of the *Chicago Tribune*'s "Woman News," which was filled with national and international content in order to be sold for syndication.

Journalists at these three newspapers present three stories about how newspaper editors and reporters create contemporary pages for women. The stories, however, are an echo of the past in more ways than just the reasoning behind creating them. The stories illustrate how a lack of commitment to these sections by upper management results in limited resources and space. They also show the conflicting feeling journalists have about these sections and the difficulties related to defining women's news. Interviews at two newspapers not constructing contemporary women's pages also show how popular the idea continues to be. In both of those cases editors have considered explicitly named women's pages. In fact, one of these newspapers essentially began producing women's pages but without the explicit title. These case studies together illustrate the relevancy of a discussion about whether to produce women's pages in U.S. newspapers nearly 120 years after they were first produced.

The decision by some editors and publishers to again segregate women's content in U.S. newspapers is especially interesting in light of the comments two editors made during this study. Both editors who work at newspapers that produce explicitly named women's sections said it would be wrong to target another audience by creating special sections as they do for women. One of the editors said it would be offensive to specifically target a Native-American audience while the other said the same about a young readership. Neither of the two editors acknowledged a contradiction related to their perspective. Why is it that editors might accept the segregation and marginalization of women readers but not another demographic group? That in the year 2002 it is seen as acceptable to marginalize and segregate women in U.S. newspapers speaks more broadly to the accepted treatment of women in all areas of our culture. That this is allowed to occur in a media product that is theoretically produced for a general geographical audience is disturbing. I find this particularly problematic because of the special position news organizations are expected to hold in a democratic society. Newspapers should be constructed to inform a community or electorate. This makes them a unique medium and one that should not separate women. These examples from my interviews show that the marginalization and unequal status of women in U.S. culture is prevalent enough in our social fabric to be seen as natural. The solution to marginalize women's content is seen as a common sense solution to the problem of a declining female readership. This dominant ideology frames women's acceptable roles and position in society as natural and therefore to marginalize women in newspapers is a natural solution to an industry-wide problem.

An essential question to ask is whether this solution to construct a section for women allows editors throughout the rest of a newspaper to operate business as usual rather than integrate women's voices and areas of interest into all sections of the newspaper. Advocates for contemporary women's pages argue that as long as our media system is male dominated, women need space of their own to define news and construct content. The reasoning is that these sections offer a place for women's voices in the newspapers and give women an opportunity to define what is important. From this perspective, the construction of these sections has allowed women to be brought to the table and to have a voice. Some would go so far as to say they are feminist because they offer a space for women. Advocates for these special sections believe that important stories found on the women's pages would not otherwise be covered in our daily newspapers. Timely news that may be thought of as most interest to women may not get published in the news sections because it is seen by editors (mostly males) in the newsroom as a "women's issue," or not seen by them at all because it is a women's issue.

Constructing Women Readers as Consumers

Both traditional and contemporary women's pages have been produced in much the same way. Women's magazines served as models for the creation of women's pages in U.S. newspapers at their initial inception during the 1890s and again when newspapers reintroduced them starting in 1989. The first women's pages were developed in 1890 and modeled after *The Ladies' Home Journal*. At each of the three newspapers I visited where explicit women's pages exist editors said they modeled their pages after popular women's magazines. Even the *Milwaukee Journal Sentinel* created its "Compass" pages (the women's pages without the explicit title) after examining popular women's magazines, including *Ms.*, a self-described feminist publication. The problem is that most women's magazines produce content with the purpose of constructing women as consumers. To rely on these periodicals to guide women's pages in newspapers reinforces women's role as consumers. This is a problem if one believes newspapers should be in the business of constructing citizens, not consumers. The implications of these sections could be construed in a rather pessimistic manner. That is, men are positioned as citizens and women as consumers.

How to define content for these pages is a problem too. To name pages for women does not set strict parameters on what content will be found on those pages. For example, the week-to-week variety illustrated when a section showcases fashion one issue and a story about feminist authors in another section; and variety in publications illustrated by the local focus at the *Lexington-Herald* and global focus in the original version of "Woman News." On any given day throughout the history of women's pages, a reader might find content that constructs women through traditional roles or presents women in progressive and alternative ways. That is an ultimate contradiction about these pages: no one really knows what "women's news" is. With this understanding comes the acknowledgment that this is content that could be in other sections of the newspaper. The obvious question then becomes: Why name it for women?

A related problem with these explicitly named women's pages is that they essentialize notions of women and women's interests. Contemporary feminism focuses attention on the diversity of women and there is certainly a danger in newspaper pages that promote essentialist notions of women through stereotypes. This is not to say that there are not gender differences in terms of what men and women say they want from a newspaper. Reader survey data suggests differences. But these are generalities and should be taken as such. To name content based on these is a dangerous and limiting decision. To publish certain stories under a "woman" label may validate some women's desires and interests but insults many women too. Further, publishing lighter topics under a sex-specific name and placing them behind the news, sports, and business sections in a newspaper indicates "women's concerns" are less important. Because by default this construction indicates that men's interests—found throughout the rest of the sections of the newspaper—are valued in these newsrooms in a way that women's are not. What results is a reaffirmation of the unequal status of women in American culture.

Critics of these sections, however, must be careful not to criticize "women's news"—or what some women express an interest in—as superficial. To do this would be to devalue what many women say they desire to read in their newspapers. It is important to remember that these sections are popular with many women readers. Too often critics prescribe what they believe to be best for women rather than acknowledging what women want. What is important to understand is that what women readers appreciate about these sections is the content, not the location of it in one section, in the back of the paper, under a gender specific heading. If women are given the opportunity to read a newspaper that covers on its front page and most every other page the issues they say they desire to read, then maybe a section targeting women once a week would not be so popular. Rather than critique the content, my criticism is aimed at newspapers that marginalize this content under a sex-specific nameplate; at newspapers that add women's pages in an attempt to gain and satisfy women readers and do not integrate women and "women's content" into all sections of the newspaper.

Feminism and Women's Pages

The relationship between women's pages and feminism is evident yet complex and contradictory as are many of the issues related to this sex-specific categorizing of news content. Social shifts during the 1890s, 1960s, and 1970s, and again during the 1980s and 1990s have corresponded to newspaper industry shifts in the construction (or at least conceptualization) of women readers. The connection between the repositioning of women in U.S. newspapers and social ideological changes in the country is most evident in how the intense feminist and social movements in the 1960s and 1970s responded to traditional women's pages and how an increasingly strong religious and conservative political movement (anti-feminist) starting in the 1980s corresponded with the reintroduction of these pages. It is worth reiterating the point that "news texts routinely emphasize meanings and values associated with those groups, which hold positions of political and economic power" but, at the same time, news texts do not produce a seamless dominant ideology (Carragee 1991, 3). Considering these ideas, it is important to consider how contemporary women's sections fit into Faludi's (1991) discussion of a backlash. Are they ultimately a reminder to keep women in their traditional places? Common memory names the 1960s and 1970s as an especially active period within the women's movement. The feminism of the last two decades, however, has the reputation—at least in the mass press and in popular culture—of being less energetic and relevant.

While cultural transformations are obviously complex, the above mentioned cultural shifts offer an explanation for why the segregation of women in U.S. newspapers was again by the 1990s seen as acceptable to many in the industry. It is not a coincidence that women's sections began to reappear at the same time that Faludi identifies a feminist backlash in U.S. society. A cultural and ideological climate allowed newspapers to reintroduce women's sections while a different ideological climate only decades earlier had forced newspapers to dissolve these gendered sections. But to call these pages a backlash might be an over simplification. The content in these sections and the re-emergence of women's sections is much too complex.

Women's pages have offered content about the everyday realties many American women face as a primary homemaker and caregiver and stories about feminism and feminist movements. They offer content about an alternative ideological perspective; they are a place where a feminist voice can repeatedly be identified in U.S. newspapers. But while content on these pages has covered feminist concerns, and many editors of these sections have either explicitly or implicitly identified with feminism, the sections present a fractured feminism at best. The sections also present content that could be considered anti-feminist, for example, the stories in the *Tribune*'s "Woman News" about women associated with the Christian Right. Further, editors at the *Chicago Tribune* consciously disassociate the section with feminism. The end result is a product that at times illuminates a feminist consciousness, yet is uneven and often fractured by stereotypical conceptions of women that are dominant in our patriarchal society.

Do Women Matter?

Women throughout the decades have had little power to define news, to construct reality, and to shape notions of gender as they have had limited access in newsrooms. But debate continues over whether women in decision-making positions in newsrooms really would change the news product. After all, some argue, journalists become socialized into the norms, values, and routines of news and all basically produce the same types of content. This study adds perspectives to this debate.

Frequently newsroom workers disagreed with recreating and working on explicitly named women's pages yet the newspaper's top executives created the sections anyway. It should not go unnoticed that it was primarily women who opposed the reintroduction of women's pages in the newsrooms studied for this book. Several editors and reporters I interviewed expressed dismay with creating women's pages yet worked on them anyway. And even those who said they eventually came around to supporting it never expressed absolute support. For example, "Woman News" columnist Barbara Brotman said her cynicism faded but "not a lot." Also, one of the "You" section's founding editors explained that she "sort of" became a convert. These statements indicate that because these women were hired to construct content for explicitly named women's pages they did. In fact, that is exactly what the women's pages editor at *The Capital Times* said. These women were never forced to comply but were willing to conform because of an interest in fitting in and/or remaining employed. Ultimately these women's concerns were ignored and they were forced to "come around" to an patriarchal way of thinking if they wanted to remain employed. This speaks to women's unequal status and illustrates another reason why it is so important that women be included in decision-making positions within newsrooms.

The question remains: would women in decision-making positions really change the news? Most of the journalists I interviewed believed that women editors and reporters choose and construct news differently. There was overwhelming consensus that individual characteristics do influence content, whether it is gender, parental status, marital status, race, or ethnicity. Many of those I interviewed believed women also possessed different sensibilities and interests and therefore created different content than men. For example, the women's section editor at *The Capital Times* illustrated how her personal background influenced her section's content through the publication of stories presented from a feminist perspective. Documentation from women in the industry—past and present—also illustrates this belief. Some, however, did say this effect is likely more prevalent and possible in feature news writing and reporting than in "hard" news reporting. This is because the routines and norms associated with the production of hard news are much more clearly defined—for example the use of official sources, balance, and inverted pyramid style. Feature content, conversely, is less clearly defined. This less restrictive form of content allows an individual reporter or editor more agency in the shaping of content. But another example, that of Diana Bacha at the *Milwaukee Journal Sentinel* resisting the naming of her new pages for women, illustrates how women in decision-making positions can influence organizational policy and hints that greater numbers of previously underrepresented groups working in decision-making roles in newsrooms can affect content.

Why It Matters

This notion of segregating or "ghettoizing" issues of importance to women is significant and the inadequate consideration to it over the years is troubling. Segregating issues believed to be of concern and interest to women reinforces age-old stereotypes about gender and a gendered public/private dichotomy. Further, it is worth repeating that marginalizing "women's interests" insinuates that they are somehow of less importance than news topics and story types found on the front pages of newspapers. Finally, these gendered sections allow men, who too often have ultimate control over newspaper content, to continue marginalizing women's news rather than integrating it. While niche marketing may be acceptable in the magazine industry, where women's periodicals are extremely popular, and on television, where shows like *Oprah* target women, this separation of the sexes in daily newspapers is problematic and dangerous for women. Newspapers hold a unique position in our cultural history—they are expected to inform citizens about the world, to aid citizens in a participatory democracy.

The positioning and repositioning of women in newspapers speaks more broadly about how women are positioned in U.S. culture. The newspaper industry, as a means of mass communication, has the power to construct and reify social meaning. In its positioning of women, general knowledge about a culture's positioning and construction of women can be gleaned. Newspapers, like other cultural objects, reflect and reinforce cultural realities, values, and beliefs. To separate "women's news" from the rest of the paper, whether it is 1890 or 1990, at best insinuates that the rest of the news—including political and economic stories—is meant for and of interest only to men. But at its worst, it explicitly states that women's news and issues (defined by journalists as pay equity, harassment in the workplace, violence against women, breaking barriers, and juggling home, family, and elder care) are not of concern to men. Do men not play a role in why women receive unequal pay for equal work? Do men not play a role in the harassment that goes on in the workplace, the violation of rape countless women endure every day, and the battering of women in their homes? Are men not responsible for the health and care of their family members both young and old? It seems ridiculous to ask these questions but it is equally ridiculous to name these as "women's news." Doing so reinforces the idea that women should care more than men about these everyday issues and that they should primarily attend to them. This positioning of issues into a sex-specific realm reflects dominant societal views but journalists should not reinforce these outdated conceptions of gender. By constructing and conceptualizing news in this manner newspapers with an explicitly named women's section both generate and circulate a notion that women are responsible for issues that are societal concerns, which should be addressed in that manner and not by half of the population. These are political and social issues that should occupy a space on the front pages and news pages of newspapers. Newspapers with women's pages run the risk of marginalizing issues that greatly affect women's and men's lives and in doing so emphasize values associated with the United States' patriarchal ideology. When free from these gendered issues men are able to dedicate their energy toward the pursuit of economic wealth and political power. In theory newspapers are meant for a general audience, established to inform and empower a community, and to aid the democratic process. In practice, newspapers that explicitly segregate "women's news" reify the inequalities of men and women and strip women of the potential power that comes with equality. Further, these newspapers play a role in the "symbolic annihilation" of women—both trivializing and erasing women through the placement of their work and stories about them on special pages rather than the front news pages.

To accept the argument that these sections are needed because women's voices and "issues" are not in other areas of the newspaper seems a defeatist position. To tolerate a women's section is to accept that men dominate the newspaper industry and to put up with women's limited ability to define news. Acknowledging a reality is one thing, accepting it is another. Supporting the newspaper industry's segregation of women's news allows those in the newspaper industry to ignore its patriarchal structure and not work toward the integration and empowerment of women. Further, it reifies social meaning about women's separate and secondary positioning in society. That many women working on these gendered sections only accepted rather than supported them underlines how little power women have in newsrooms.

The decline of female readership has caused U.S. newspapers to come up with specific—if maybe not so innovative—ways to appeal to this segment of the population. But the problems critics pointed to with the original women's pages have not disappeared. The concern with these sections is the same as it was in the 1960s and 1970s. Ultimately, the consequences associated with contemporary newspapers offering women's pages are too risky. They let newspaper publishers, editors, and reporters off the hook, letting them believe they are giving women something special when what women need is to be treated with respect. To be given space for their voices and their concerns throughout newspapers. This is not to dismiss women and men's real and/or perceived differences but to say that women's interests—if they really are different from men's—should be equally represented in all sections of the paper.

Clearly there is a better way to offer women content than to marginalize it into a weekly section located at the back of the paper. The *Lexington Herald-Leader*'s approach (and the Knight-Ridder report written in the late 1980s that recommends a holistic solution to the problem of declining female readers) shows promise. The success the *Herald-Leader* had in attracting women readers illustrates how, through a complex approach, newspapers can win back women readers. Newspapers must place women in decision-making roles. Like at the *Herald-Leader*, editors must promote changing the whole paper and constantly place "women's news" into all areas of their product. Whether or not people agree that a women's section is an important and needed aspect of a contemporary newspaper, few would argue against the idea of integrating women's voices into all areas of the paper or against hiring more women into decision-making positions in the newsroom. Only one of the three newspapers I visited took this holistic approach to righting the problem of women's content and voices and declining readership.

Rather than introduce a special section for women, newspapers should focus on what the *Lexington Herald-Leader* did—bring more women into decision-making positions and put women's voices and "issues" on the front page and throughout the paper. Reader surveys indicate this strategy actually worked to gain women readers. In fact it was the only paper of the three that had marketing data showing a rise in its female readership after producing contemporary women's pages.

The Future of Women's Pages

The number of U.S. newspapers that added or considered producing contemporary women's pages during the 1990s indicated an industry-wide concern. Whether to include explicitly named women pages continued to be a topic of debate even as the 1990s came to an end. In 1998 *Los Angeles Times* executives dealing with a half-million gap in female readers of their daily versus Sunday paper were contemplating adding a special section for women (Miller 1998). While the *Times* has yet to unveil such a section, its concern in attracting women readers was clear. This book offers telling information to the newspaper industry. By chronicling the *Lexington Herald-Leader*'s story and illustrating how the newspaper was able to regain women readers, the book offers newspapers a way to solve the problem of a declining readership while making a case against the marginalization of content of interest to women into special sections.

But what seemed especially important in the 1990s seems less so today as the newspaper industry faces a declining readership across demographics. Even as I conducted my interviews, it was clear that rather than women newspaper executives were growing more concerned about attracting and keeping young readers. However, ironically, *Lexington Herald-Leader* publisher Tim Kelly said to create pages targeting teens would not be the answer to his paper's new "at-risk" reading audience. The reason: the solution would be offensive and exclusionary. Since my interviews, not only has the *Lexington-Herald* eliminated its women's pages, so has the *Chicago Tribune*. In 2002 the paper instituted a subtle shift, replacing the "Woman News" nameplate with "WN." Then in December 2005, the *Tribune* stopped publishing "Woman News."

Still, newspapers continue to try these segregated sections—though it is quite difficult to determine how many are doing so. One way this segregation is now happening in on news websites, rather than in print editions. Will we see the end of women's pages in newspapers? One can only hope and this research offers reason for hope. That the *Lexington Herald-Leader* moved beyond a women's section and made an effort to weave women into all areas of the newsroom and content of the paper is significant. Perhaps more noteworthy, the *Chicago Tribune* has abandoned its sex-specific pages. Further, most U.S. newspapers disregarded the trend to create women's pages. Also, encouraging is that even where high-level editors wanted women's pages, lower-level editors like Diana Bacha were able to resist the explicit naming of those pages for women. This is a small victory but a victory nonetheless. That evidence has not shown women's pages to actually attract women readers could contribute to their continued elimination, though this research suggests that other newspapers may try them but that they will not have a long production life. As more women move into high-level decision-making positions in newsrooms across the country, the sections may become less popular as well since women in the newsrooms I visited were more likely to resist or even despise them. This resistance has much to do with the sections reminding women of the past and of their historically marginalized status in U.S. culture. Further evidence of "women's pages" vulnerable status in the industry is the fact that the majority of U.S. newspapers remain committed to offering sex-neutral feature pages.

Competition between newspapers, however, increases the pressure to attract target audiences and newspaper executives will continue to try old and new ideas to get readers. But as I stated, women readers are currently less of a worry for newspaper executives. The bigger worry is much grander—how to get new and keep old readers. While over the decades competition between newspapers has decreased competition between mediums—television, magazines and more recently the Internet—have placed more pressure than ever on newspapers to gain valuable audience members. A particular concern in the industry is the use of Web news by a growing number of teenagers and young adults. The fast changes currently occurring in the news industry and brought on by new technologies mean news organizations rather than newspapers must now consider how to conceptualize a female readership and construct content for them in a new media environment. The charge of journalism, however, remains the same—to inform citizens. But journalists cannot do this outside of an industry that relies on consumers. Will the news Web sites, through the placement and designation of content, continue to reinforce the notion that men are citizens and women are consumers? It seems a number of news Web sites are creating a special section for "women's news" and making that explicit through its title. How much will change for women journalists and readers, then, in this new environment? And when will "women's news" stop being women's news?

References

Abramson, Phyllis L. 1990. *Sob sister journalism*. New York: Greenwood Press.

Beasley, Maurine H. and Sheila J. Gibbons. 2003. *Taking their place: a documentary history of women and journalism,* 2nd ed. State College, PA: Strata Publishing.

Becker, S. 1984. Marxist approaches to media studies: the British experience. *Critical Studies in Mass Communication* 1:66–80.

Behar, R. 1996. *The vulnerable observer: anthropology that breaks your heart.* Boston: Beacon.

Belford, B. 1986. *Brilliant bylines.* New York: Columbia University Press.

Braden, M. 1991. Women: special again. *Washington Journalism Review.* June 13:30–32.

Branson, Craig. 2002. A look at the formation of ASNE. http://www.asne.org/index.cfm?ID=3460 (accessed February 6, 2003).

Bridge, J. 1995. Men mostly missing from coverage of parental issues. *The Quill* Nov./Dec.:18.

Cairns, Kathleen A. 2003. *Front-page women journalists, 1920–1950.* Lincoln: University of Nebraska Press.

Carragee, K. M. 1991. News and ideology: an analysis of coverage of the west German Green Party by *The New York Times. Journalism Monographs* 128: 1–30.

Castleberry, Vivian. 1989. Women in journalism (interview), Washington Press Club Foundation, session 2, http://npc.press.org (accessed June 5, 2005).

Chambers, Deborah, Linda Steiner, and Carole Fleming. 2004. *Women and journalism.* New York: Routledge.

Collins, Jean E. 1980. *She was there: stories of pioneering women journalists.* Julian Messner: New York.

Collins, Patricia H. 1990. *Black feminist thought: knowledge, consciousness and the politics of empowerment.* New York: Routledge, Chapman & Hall.

Cox, J. 1992. Newspapers court women. *USA Today* November 24:B8.

Cuklanz, Lisa M. 1996. *Rape on trial: how the mass media construct legal reform and social change.* Philadelphia: University of Pennsylvania Press.

Danner, L. and S. Walsh. 1999. "Radical" feminists and "bickering" women: backlash in U.S. media coverage of the United Nations Fourth World Conference on Women. *Critical Studies in Mass Communication* 16:63–84.

Denzin, Norman K. 1989. *Interpretive interactionism.* Newbury Park, CA: Sage.

Dishon, K. 1997. We've come a long way, maybe. *Media Studies Journal* 11(2): 92–101.

Donovan, Josephine. 1994. *Feminist theory: the intellectual traditions of American feminism.* New York: Continuum.

Editor & Publisher. 1970. Favorite reading matter for women covers wide area. Oct.: 13.

Editor & Publisher. 1971. How they would liberate the women's pages from drab content. May 1:9–11.

Endres, Kathleen L. and Therese L. Lueck, eds. 1995. *Women's periodicals in the United States: consumer magazines.* Westport, CT: Greenwood Press.

Faludi, Susan. 1991. *Backlash: the undeclared war against American women.* New York: Doubleday.

Ferguson, Marjorie. 1983. *Forever feminine: women's magazines and the cult of femininity.* London: Heinemann.

Fink, C. C. 1989. How newspapers should handle upscale/downscale conundrum. *Presstime* March:40–41.

Fiske, John. 1987. *Television culture.* London: Routledge.

———. 1992. "British cultural studies and television." In *Channels of discourse, reassembled,* edited by R. C. Allen. Chapel Hill: University of North Carolina Press.

Fontana, Andrea and James Frey. 2000. "The interview: from structured questions to negotiated text." In *Handbook of qualitative research,* 2nd ed., edited by N. K. Denzin and Y. S. Lincoln. Thousand Oaks, CA: Sage.

Fost, D. 1991. Newspapers are teaching targeting. *American Demographics.* May 13:18–19.

Gitlin, Todd. 1980. *The whole world is watching.* Berkeley: University of California Press.

Goodman. E. 1993. Symposium – Is the media a woman's place. *Media Studies Journal: The Media and Women without Apology* 7(1–2):49–67.

Gramsci, A. 1971. *Selections from the prison notebooks of Antonio Gramsci.* Edited and translated by Q. Hoare & G. Smith. New York: International Publishers.

Greenwald. Marilyn S. 1999. *A woman of the Times.* Athens: Ohio University Press.

Guenin, Zena Beth. 1975. Women's pages in American newspapers: missing out on contemporary content. *Journalism Quarterly* 52:66–75.

Hansen, M. 1992. Reconcilable differences? *News Inc.* Sept.:23–28.

Hartley, John. 1982. *Understanding news.* London: Methuen.

Hawley, Melinda. 1997. *Is the "Women's Section" an anachronism: affinity for and ambivalence about the* Chicago Tribune's WomaNews. Paper present at the Association for Education in Journalism and Mass Communication, Chicago, August.

Holland, Patricia. 1998. "The politics of the smile." In *News, Gender and Power,* edited by C. Carter et. al. New York: Routledge.

Jackson, N. B. 1993. *1990s women's news: the roots.* Paper presented to the Commission on the Status of Women, Association for Education in Journalism & Mass Communication, Kansas City, MO, August.

Jordan, Elizabeth. 1938. *Three rousing cheers.* New York: Appleton-Century.

Jurney, D. 1982. Men (mostly) still in charge, but more women are on the way. *The Bulletin* Nov.:3–5.

Kelly, C. 1993. The great paper chase: losing women readers, the dailies try to win us back. *Ms.* May/June:34–35.

Kelly, S. 1972. Editors: don't drop women from paper's women's pages. *Editor & Publisher* July 15:30, 32, 34.

Kitch, Carolyn. 2002. "Women in journalism." In *American Journalism: History, Principles, Practices* edited by Sloan, W. David and Lisa Mullikin Parcell. Jefferson, NC: McFarland.

Krolokke, Charlotte and Anne Scott Sorensen. 2006. *Gender communication theories and analyses*. Thousand Oaks, CA: Sage.

Lentz, R. M. 1975. What's this "Women's Editor" to do? *The Quill* Feb.:29.

Liebler, C. M. and S. J. Smith. 1997. Tracking gender differences: a comparative analysis of network correspondence and their sources. *Journal of Broadcasting and Electronic Media* 41:58–68.

Long, C. 1972. The A. J. Liebling counter-convention colossus. *The Quill* June: 34, 37.

Lont, Cynthia. 1995. *Women and media: content/careers/criticism*. Belmont, CA: Wadsworth.

Lueck, Therese and Huayun Chang. 2002. Tribune's 'WomaNews' gives voice to women's issues, *Newspaper Research Journal* 23(1):59–72.

Maeglin, K. 1995. TCT's new Savvy has something for everyone. *Capital Times* Sept. 7, p. F1.

Marzolf, Marion T. 1977. *Up from the footnote: a history of women journalists*. New York: Hasting House.

Media and Gender Monitor. 1998. The women's page: Godsend or ghetto? http://www.aworc.org/bpfa/pub/sec_j/com00002.html (accessed on March 16, 2001).

Merritt, S. and H. Gross. 1978. Women's page/lifestyle editors: does sex make a difference? *Journalism Quarterly* 55:508–514.

Mills, Kay. 1988. *A place in the news: from the women's pages to the front page*. New York: Dodd, Mead.

Miller, S. 1976. Changes in women's/lifestyle sections. *Journalism Quarterly* 53: 641–647.

———. 1985. Was "Pink Collar" ghetto study deliberate sensationalism? *Editor & Publisher* Nov. 23:52.

———. 1989. The latest editorial challenge is to regain women readers. *ASNE Bulletin* Sept.:8–12.

———. 1993. Opportunity squandered — newspapers and women's news. *Media Studies Journal: The Media and Women without Apology* 7(1–2):167–182.

———. 1998. Women and content. *Presstime* April:41–45.

Oakley, Ann. 1974. *The sociology of housework*. New York: Pantheon.

———. 1981. "Interviewing women: a contradiction in terms." In *Doing feminist research* edited by H. Roberts. London: Routledge & Kegan Paul.

Pearl, D. 1992. Newspapers strive to win women back. *The Wall Street Journal* May 4, p. B1.

Penney-Missouri Awards. 1970. Banquet program titled: Penney-Missouri awards: 10th anniversary 1960–1970.

Press, A. L. 1993. Feminist methodology? A reassessment. *Contemporary Sociology* Jan.:23–29.

Rapping, Elayne. 1994. *Media-tions: forays into the culture and gender wars*. Boston: South End Press.

Roesgen, J. 1972. How much relevance can a woman take? *The Bulletin*. Feb.: 4-5.

Ryan, Barbara. 1992. *Feminism and the women's movement: dynamics of change in social movement, ideology and activism*. New York: Routledge.

Schlipp, Madelon Golden and Sharon M. Murphy. 1983. *Great women of the press*. Carbondale: Southern Illinois Press.

Schmidt, K. and C. Collins. 1993. Showdown at gender gap. *American Journalism Review* July/Aug.:39–42.

Schudson, Michael. 1978. *Discovering the news: a social history of American newspapers.* New York: Basic Books.

———. 1989. The sociology of news production. *Media, Culture and Society* 11: 263–282.

Scott, J. 1974. Women's page changes noted by three editors. *Editor & Publisher* July 6:21.

Shoemaker, P. J. 1984. Media treatment of deviant political groups. *Journalism Quarterly* 61(1):66–75.

Shoemaker, Pamela J. and Stephen D. Reese. 1991. *Mediating the message: theories of influence on mass media content.* New York: Longman.

Steiner, L. 1997. Gender at work: early accounts by women journalists. *Journalism History* 23(1):2–15

Streitmatter, Rodger. 1994. *Raising her voice: African-American women journalists who changed history.* Lexington: University Press of Kentucky.

———. 1998. Transforming the women's pages: strategies that worked. *Journalism History* 24(2):72–81.

Tuchman, Gaye. 1978. *Making News.* New York: The Free Press.

Tuchman, Gaye, Arlene Kaplan Daniels, and James Benet, eds. 1978. *Hearth and Home: Images of Women in the Mass Media.* New York: Oxford University Press.

Van Gelder, L. 1974. Women's pages: you can't make news out of a silk purse. *Ms.* November:112–126.

Von Hoffman, N. 1971. Women's pages: an irreverent view. *Columbia Journalism Review* July/Aug:52–54.

Van Zoonen, Liesbet. 1994. *Feminist media studies.* London: Sage.

———. 1998. "One of the girls? The changing gender of journalism." In *News, Gender and Power* edited by Cynthia Carter, Gill Branston, and Stuart Allan. New York: Routledge.

Voss, K. W. 2006. The Penney-Missouri awards: honoring the best in women's news. *Journalism History* 32(1):43–50.

Walker, Nancy A. 1998. Women's magazines 1940–1960: gender roles and the popular press. Boston: Bedford/St. Martin's.

———. 2000. *Shaping our mothers' world: American women's magazines.* Jackson: University Press of Mississippi.

Welter, B. 1966. The cult of true womanhood: 1820–1860. *American Quarterly* 18:151–174.

Williamson, L. 1971. Less chronicle, more guide: women's page style changed. *Editor & Publisher* Sept. 11:43–44.

Williamson, L. 1975. Workshoppers question lines dividing news, people pages. *Editor & Publisher* April 12:30, 32, 38.

Women in Journalism Washington Press Club Foundation Oral History Project. 1998. http://npc.press.org/wpforal/ohhome.htm (accessed on January 12, 2003).

Yang, M. 1996. Women's pages or people's pages: the production of news for women in the *Washington Post* in the 1950s. *Journalism & Mass Communication Quarterly* 73(2):364–378.

Zuckerman, Mary Ellen. 1998. *A history of popular women's magazines in the United States, 1792–1995.* Westport, CT: Greenwood Press.

Interview Participants

Anderson, Paula. (2002, February 19). Head of Human Resources. *Lexington Herald-Leader*.

Bacha, Diana. (2002, February 4). Assistant Managing Editor of Features/ Entertainment. *Milwaukee Journal Sentinel*.

Bergin, Mary. (2001, September 27). Features Editor. *The Capital Times*.

Brotman, Barbara. (2002, February 6). Woman News Columnist. *Chicago Tribune*.

Brown, Geoff. (2002, February 6). Associate Managing Editor of Features. *Chicago Tribune*.

Carr-Elsing, Debra. (2001, September 27). "Savvy" Writer. *The Capital Times*.

DeBaun, John. (2002, February 8). Deputy Features Editor. *Milwaukee Journal Sentinel*.

Deniro, Mary. (2001, September 27). Advertising Manager. *The Capital Times*.

Denton, Frank. (2002, January 28). Editor. *Wisconsin State Journal*.

Dunn, Bill. (2001, September 27). "Savvy" Writer. *The Capital Times*.

Elsen, Fran. (2002, February 19). Advertising Supervisor. *Lexington Herald-Leader*.

Elson, Mary. (2002, February 6). Associate Managing Editor of Features. *Chicago Tribune*.

Franz, Janet. (2002, February 6). Editor of Special Sections. *Chicago Tribune*.

Frink, Clayton. (2001, September 26). Publisher. *The Capital Times*.

Grimes, Ledatta. (2002, February 20). Features Reporter. *Lexington Herald-Leader*.

Hall, Dionne. (2002, February 20). Market Research Manager. *Lexington Herald-Leader*.

Haslanger, Phil. (2001, September 26). Managing Editor. *The Capital Times*.

Henry, Amanda. (2002, January 27). Arts Reporter. *Wisconsin State Journal*.

Higgins, Jim. (2002, February 8). Assistant Entertainment/ Features Editor. *Milwaukee Journal Sentinel*.

Johnson, Mike. (2002, February 19). Assistant Managing Editor. *Lexington Herald-Leader*.

Joyce, Denise. (2002, February 6). Health and Family Section Editor. *Chicago Tribune*.

Juzwik, Chris. (2002, January 27). Features Editor. *Wisconsin State Journal*.

Kallio, Sandy. (2002, January 27). Assistant Features Editor. *Wisconsin State Journal*.

Kelly, Tim. (2002, February 19). Publisher. *Lexington Herald-Leader*.

Leroux, Charles. (2002, February 6). Senior Writer. *Chicago Tribune*.

Mertz, Amy. (2001, September 26). "Savvy" Editor. *The Capital Times*.

Navratil, Wendy. (2002, February 6). Woman News Editor. *Chicago Tribune*.

Patrick, Kelli. (2002, February 19). Assistant Features Editor. *Lexington Herald-Leader*.

Rogers, Nicole. (2002, January 28). Assistant Features Editor. *Wisconsin State Journal*.

Rudolph, Jean. (2002, February 6). Magazine Editor. *Chicago Tribune.*

Scherer, Sally. (2002, February 20). Assistant Features Editor. *Lexington Herald-Leader.*

Uebelherr, Jan. (2002, February 4). Features Reporter. *Milwaukee Journal Sentinel.*

Wethal, Todd. (2002, February 19). Features Editor. *Lexington Herald-Leader.*

Williams, Jill. (2002, February 4). Senior Editor/Daily Features and Entertainment. *Milwaukee Journal Sentinel.*

Zweifel, Dave. (2001, September 26). Editor. *The Capital Times.*

Index

About the Author

Dustin Harp is an assistant professor in the School of Journalism at the University of Texas at Austin. She received a doctoral degree in mass communication at the University of Wisconsin, Madison. Her teaching and research interests focus on women, journalism, and women's access to public spheres through various forms of mass media. A native of California, where she got her start as a journalist, Harp teaches graduate courses in critical and cultural media theories and qualitative methods. She also teaches undergraduate courses in reporting and news design and a class on women's history in journalism and relationship to news. Harp's research has been published in a variety of communication journals.